Eric Dana

exploring mars

Mars eclipses the Sun. From one of the
moons of Mars this is what you would see

exploring mars

BY ROY A. GALLANT

ILLUSTRATED BY LOWELL HESS

GARDEN CITY BOOKS, GARDEN CITY, NEW YORK

FOR MARK

The author's thanks to Lloyd Motz,
Associate Professor of Astronomy, Columbia University,
for his helpful suggestions
regarding the manuscript of this book.

Acknowledgment is made for the quotation used from "Invasion From Mars," by Howard Koch (Orson Welles broadcast of H. G. Wells' "The War Of The Worlds") copyright 1940, by Princeton University Press. By arrangement with Monica McCall, Inc.

LIBRARY OF CONGRESS CATALOG CARD NUMBER 55–12238

contents

map of mars

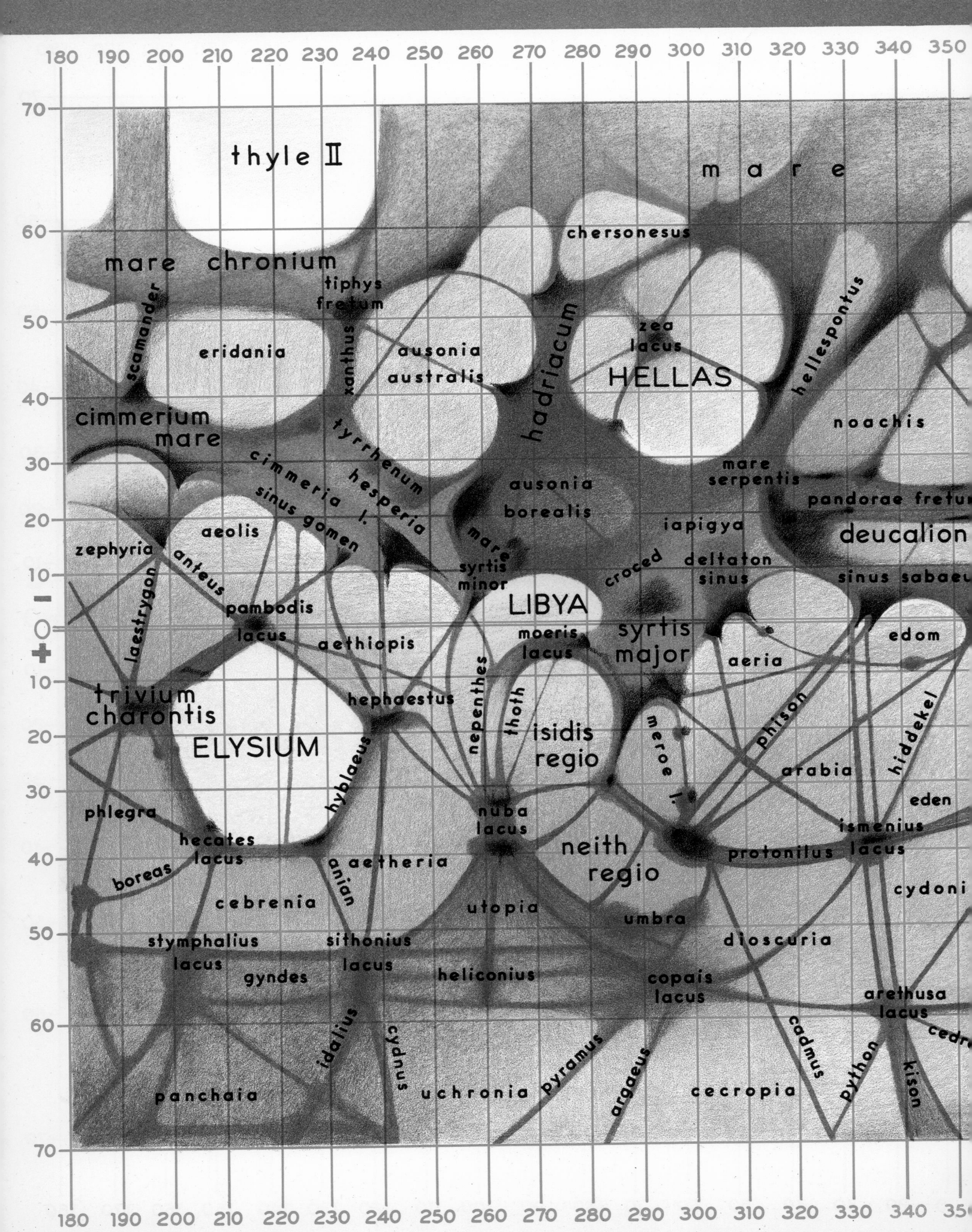

seas, deserts have Latin and Greek names.
Map is based on Antoniadi's observations.

Thin cross-lines are "canals" which many
astronomers say are visible on Red Planet.

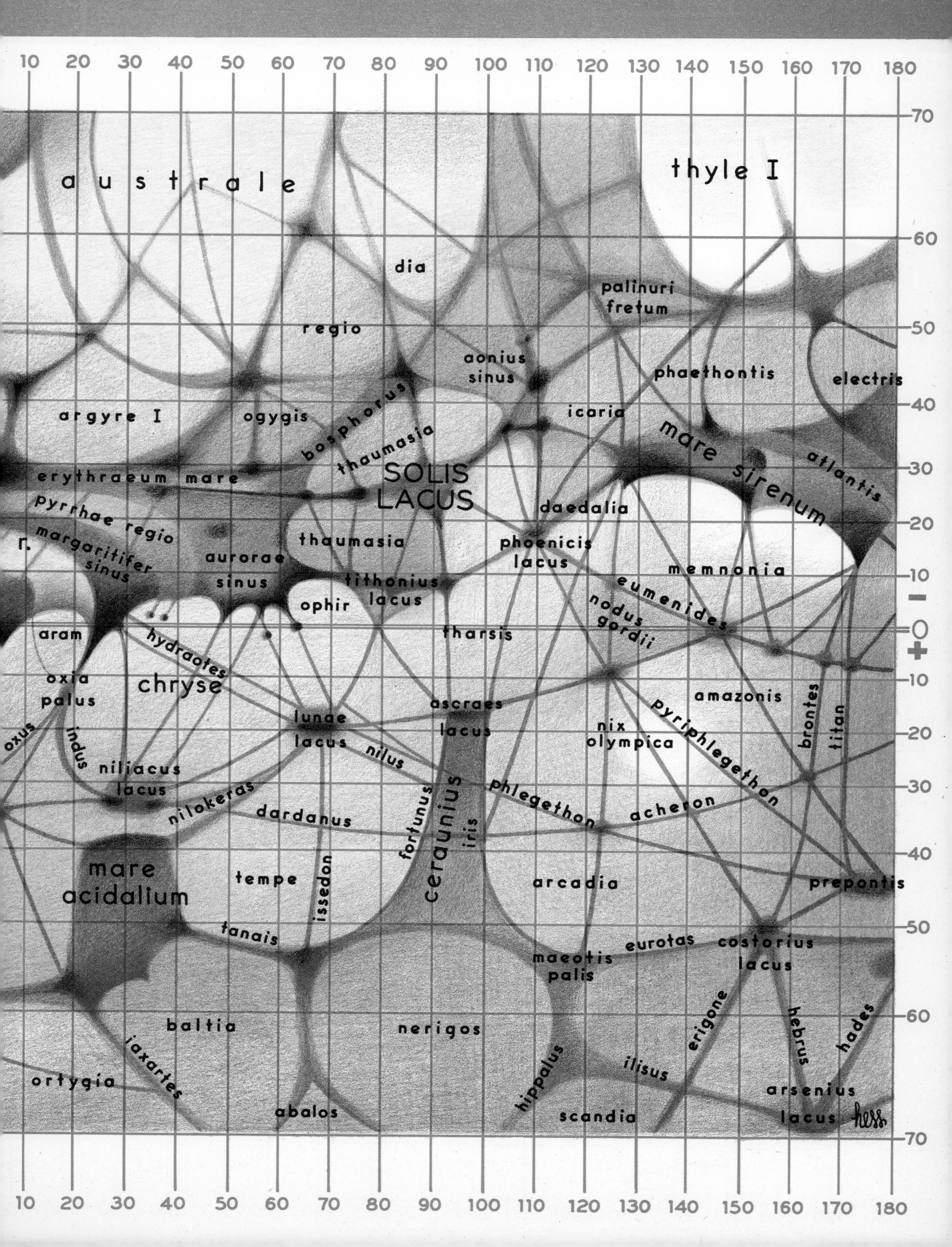

the mystery planet

For more than 300 years astronomers the world over have been trying to solve the mystery of the Red Planet, Mars. Ever since men first turned their inquiring eyes toward the heavens, Mars caught their attention and fired their imagination. They thought of Mars as a "special" member of the Sun's family of planets.

One reason is that Mars is a close neighbor—barely a stone's throw away when we consider the vast distances of outer space. And because it is so close, through the ages men have wondered, "Can Mars really be *very* different from our own planet? And is it *too* farfetched to suppose there may be intelligent beings on Mars?"

Unlike the other planets which shine from bright to dim white, Mars is an orange-red color and so has earned its nickname, the "Red Planet." But it deserves still another nickname—the "Mystery Planet." For even with the wealth of knowledge our great telescopes have given us, there is still little we can say about Mars with certainty.

The astronomer is interested in Mars because it is the best planetary target for his telescope. When Mars passes close to Earth (and by "close" the astronomer means about forty million miles), the eye can penetrate the planet's thin veil of atmosphere and pick out hundreds of intriguing features. Many of these features have been photographed and drawn and then pieced together in the form of a map of the planet. For years astronomers have been observing Mars and have been hard at work mapping its orange deserts, its great mysterious blue-green areas, its gleaming white polar caps, its elusive canals, and other queer markings.

9

They have even figured out a Martian calendar which, strangely enough, is even more accurate than our own Earth calendar. They have discovered many things about the planet's atmosphere. They have measured the temperatures of Martian summer days, which are comfortably warm, and of the bitter winter nights, which are paralyzingly cold. They have even given names to many of its areas—names such as Utopia, Lake of the Sun, the Sea of Serpents, and the Gulf of Pearls. But in spite of the many books and hundreds of technical papers written about Mars, much of our knowledge about the Red Planet is uncertain. To prove this for yourself, all you have to do is read two or three technical books about Mars and see how even the experts have come to grips with each other.

For example, the Red Planet's mysterious "canals" have been one of the most hotly debated topics in recent astronomy. At one time some people thought they were extensive man-made waterways. Now there are astronomers who say that the canal-like markings don't exist at all. Their true nature probably won't be solved until the first space ship lands on Mars to give scientists a close-up view.

One reason for the many debates about Mars is the difficulty astronomers have in seeing the planet clearly. Even when the largest telescopes are turned on Mars when the "seeing" is excellent, the planet appears only a little larger than the full Moon as seen by the naked eye. Also, consider that to see Mars' surface the eye must first look through Earth's dense atmosphere, which is constantly in motion and so causes a "twinkling," then through Mars' atmosphere, and you'll understand why there is no such thing as a clear, detailed view of the planet. If it were possible to create a large air-free tunnel from Earth to Mars, one of the major viewing problems would be solved.

You might suggest that astronomers save on eyestrain by taking photographs of Mars, enlarge them, and so put an end to the viewing problem. Unhappily it isn't quite so easy. Like the Moon, Mars shines by light reflected from the Sun. It doesn't generate its own light as the stars do. Because the planet is so dimly lighted it is difficult to photograph. To take a good photograph you must make a time exposure. And here is where the trouble begins.

Whenever you make a time exposure, the motion of the Earth's atmosphere blurs details which might be sharp were there no atmosphere to contend with. For this reason the best maps of Mars are made not from

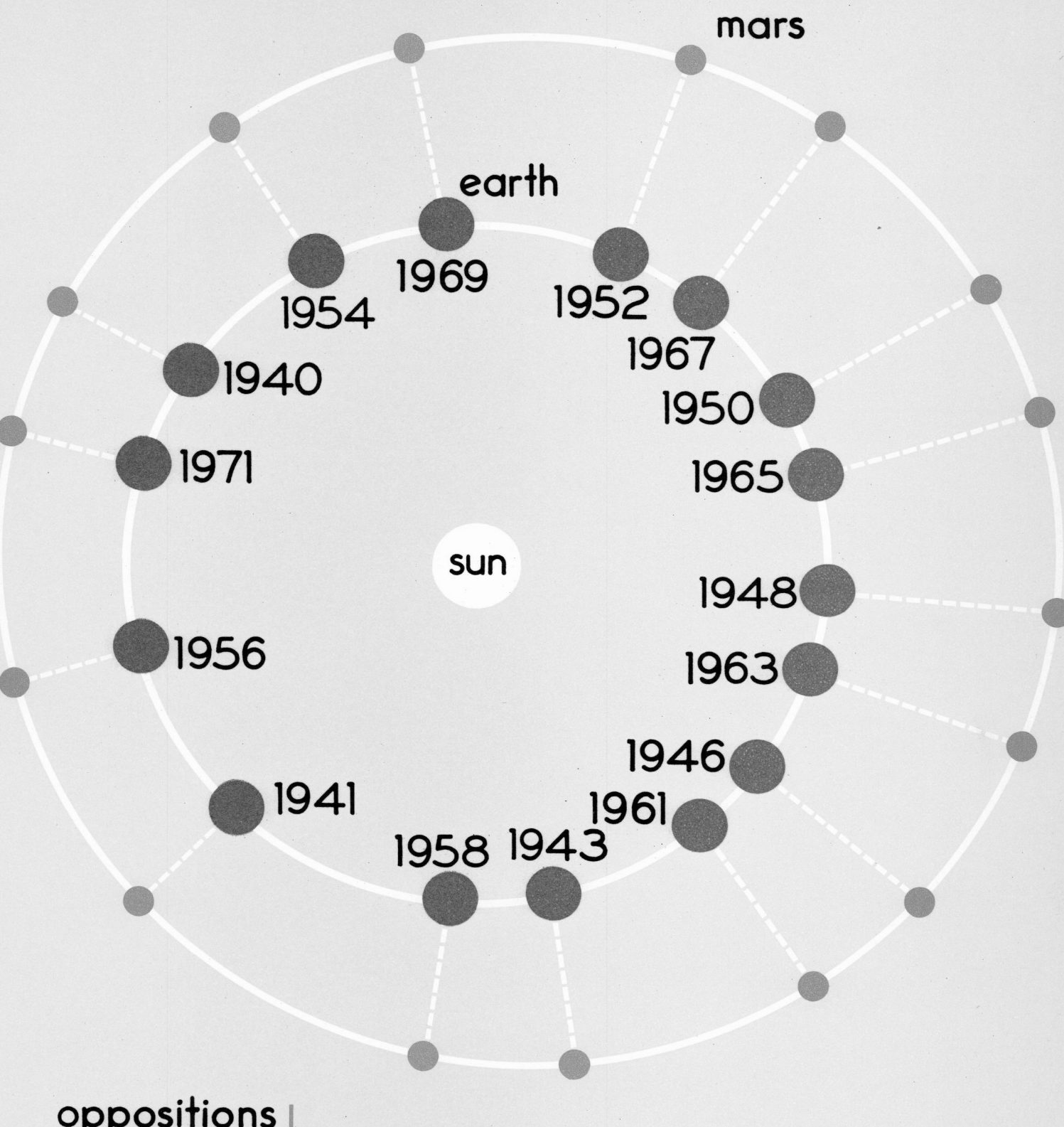

mars

earth

1969

1954

1952

1940

1967

1950

1971

1965

sun

1948

1963

1956

1946

1961

1941

1958 1943

oppositions of mars and earth

Inner and outer circles show paths of Earth and Mars. When the two planets come close, as in 1956, astronomers see Mars most clearly. Chart shows close approaches from 1940 through 1971.

photographs but from drawings done by expert observers. Drawings, however, present a special problem of their own. What one observer sees and records may not be seen quite the same way by other observers. A good example of this problem is the Red Planet's canals. While dozens of astronomers claim to have seen them clearly, others say that for years they have been looking but have never once seen anything resembling a canal.

Generally, only the finer details of the surface of Mars are open to argument. Drawings and photographs alike are in agreement about the outlines of the more prominent features—for instance, the polar caps, deserts, and the great dark regions which stretch hundreds of miles across the planet's surface. Both the eye and the camera report the same thing in these cases.

By now you may begin to understand why Mars is cloaked in mystery. It is just close enough to encourage investigation but just far enough away to make investigation difficult. Even so, each time the planet swings near Earth on its way around the Sun we manage to learn a little more about it.

This brings us now to the Red Planet's status in the family of planets. As we all know, the planets in the solar system are constantly moving around the Sun in sweeping paths called ellipses. They all move at different speeds. The speeds of Mars and Earth are such that Earth is constantly pursuing and passing Mars in a game of celestial tag. Once every two years and two months Earth passes Mars and so gives us a close-up view of the Red Planet. At such times Mars is said to be in "opposition."

Because the orbit of Mars is not a perfect circle, the planet swings exceptionally close to us every fifteen and seventeen years. Astronomers consider these oppositions choice times to observe the planet. The most recent really close approach of Mars took place on September 7, 1956. At that time the planet was only 35,160,000 miles away. To see it so close again you will have to wait until August 1971. The timetable below shows the most recent close oppositions of Mars.

YEAR	MARS' DISTANCE FROM EARTH
1939	36,000,000 miles
1954	39,800,000 miles
1956	35,160,000 miles
1971	35,000,000 miles

Whenever the Red Planet swings exceptionally close to Earth, astronomers the world over keep a nightly vigil on the planet. As a result, during each opposition they come up with new evidence which helps answer some of the more exciting questions that keep the Red Planet behind a thin veil of mystery. Some of these questions are:

Is there life on Mars?

What, actually, are the mysterious "canals"? Are they the remains of giant waterways built thousands of years ago by intelligent beings who were members of a great civilization now dead? Or are they nothing more than curious natural formations on the planet's surface? Or could they really be optical illusions, tricks the eyes play on us as we look across millions of miles of space?

What are the planet's great dark areas that change in size, shape, and color every year? Are they really large areas of plant life? If so, does this mean that animal life may exist on Mars?

And what about Mars' great polar caps? Are they thick deposits of ice like Earth's North and South poles? Or are they simply thin blankets of snow only a few inches deep?

These are only a few of the tantalizing questions about Mars that have excited the imaginations of men of science for many years. In the pages that follow we will try to answer these questions. And by so doing we will explore the work and dreams of some of the world's outstanding scientists, men who have devoted their lives in an attempt to unveil one of the most challenging mysteries of the universe—what is on the Red Planet?

Tycho leads the way

Tycho Brahe, a Danish astronomer who never owned a telescope, is one of the most colorful men of science the world has ever known. It was Tycho who made the first accurate observations of Mars and, by so doing, laid the groundwork for later astronomers. But few of his followers pursued their work with as much energy and imagination.

Born and reared a nobleman, Tycho was torn between two worlds. He enjoyed the social comfort and wealth that came with a high station in life. But he frowned on what he regarded as the "useless" lives most noblemen led. He wanted his life to have purpose; he wanted to do something worth while.

In 1562, at the age of sixteen, he was shipped off to the University of Leipzig. His father wanted him to study law, a "proper" profession for a young nobleman. But Tycho had different ideas.

In comparison with the wealth of wonders offered by the mysterious heavens, Tycho found studying law dull. Every evening as his tutor slept, Tycho put aside his law books and turned his attention to the stars, which he observed and measured secretly. A globe and a pair of compasses were the only instruments he had. Yet even with these crude tools he found errors in the work of the experts of his day. These discoveries helped convince Tycho that he was destined to be an astronomer, not a lawyer.

One night in 1572 while Tycho was observing the stars, he noticed something odd in the constellation Cassiopeia. It was a nova, a star which for some reason unknown to scientists explodes and becomes intensely bright for a few months. For several weeks the nova was so bright

that Tycho could see it in the daytime. For a year he patiently watched the nova, making notes of its brightness and position. Finally, when it disappeared, Tycho published a report of the star's behavior. At first he hesitated, thinking that publishing might be beneath his dignity, but friends convinced him that his year's work was valuable and should be made known to the world. In the final chapter of his book Tycho couldn't refrain from taking a dig or two at the "useless" lives led by noblemen. He criticized "certain people" who waste their time in sport and comparing notes of their ancestry. Such remarks had no proper place in a book on astronomy, but they probably made Tycho feel better.

The next and perhaps most important event in Tycho's life took place in 1576, when he was thirty years old. He had won the favor of Denmark's King Frederick II, who believed in Tycho's work. To show his appreciation the King gave Tycho an island, built him an observatory equipped with the finest instruments, erected a small castle for Tycho to live in, and even paid him an annual salary. There was only one thing missing. The observatory had no telescope. But this didn't disturb Tycho, because the telescope hadn't been invented yet and wasn't to be invented until after the noble astronomer's death.

Tycho's observatory was named Uraniborg, which means "fortress of the heavens." The next twenty years were probably the happiest of Tycho's life. On clear evenings when he gazed at his precious stars he dressed in his finest robes. For Tycho, astronomy was more than a profession; it was something to be regarded with great formality and respect.

During his years at Uraniborg, Tycho's stargazing helped solve many astronomical riddles. Among his more important findings were irregularities in the Moon's motion. And it was Tycho's exacting record of Mars that enabled one of his bright students, Johannes Kepler, to develop the three laws explaining how the planets move. These laws became one of the most important scientific discoveries of all times because they gave mathematical proof that the Sun, not the Earth, is the body around which the planets revolve. Even during Tycho's day people thought that the Earth was the center of the solar system.

16 Tycho Brahe died at the age of fifty-five, in the year 1601. In a way it's sad that he died before the telescope was invented. For he never saw his beloved stars in their full glory, as they are revealed by the telescope. It is also sad that not a single Martian desert or canal was named after

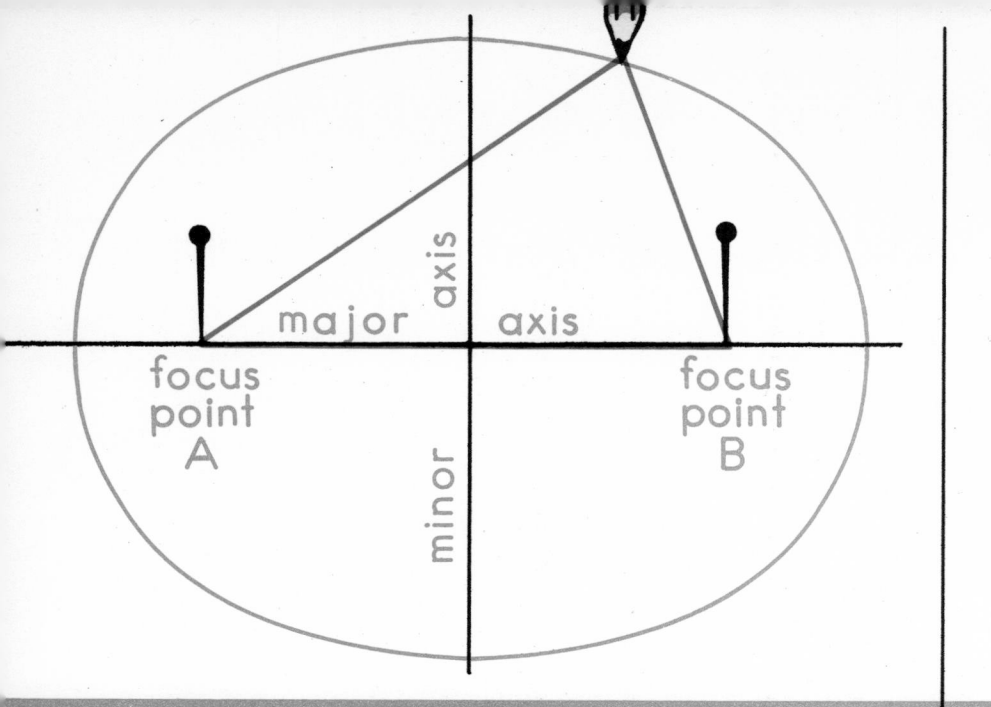

major axis

minor axis

focus point A

focus point B

the ellipse

Kepler's first law says orbits of all planets are "ellipses." To draw an ellipse, stick two pins (A and B) in a hard surface. Next drop loose loop of string over pins. With a pencil trace ellipse by letting string guide pencil around the points A and B in diagram.

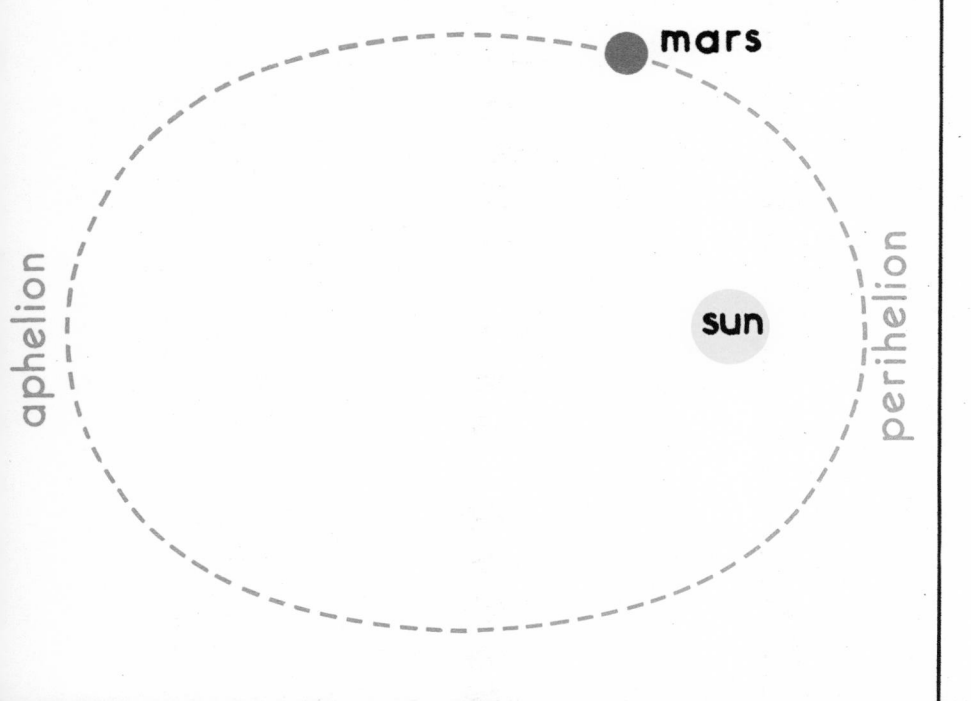

mars

sun

aphelion

perihelion

1

As shown in diagram, Kepler said that all planets travel in ellipses; also that the Sun is one of the two points (foci) that determine ellipse's shape.

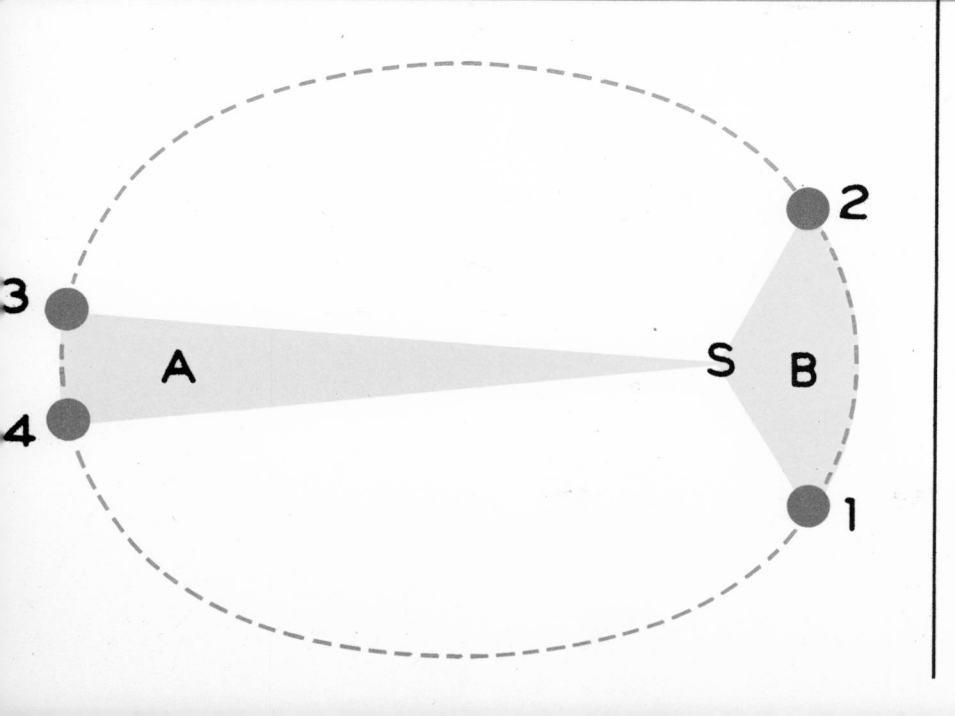

3

4

A

S B

2

1

2

Kepler's second law says that the line joining the planet to the Sun travels over equal areas in same lengths of time. In diagram, planet travels from 1 to 2 in same time as from 3 to 4.

Tycho. But perhaps he wouldn't be too offended, since the most spectacular crater on the Moon bears his name.

Tycho's followers

The invention of the telescope is what really sent Martian astronomy on its way. But oddly enough, it wasn't until about fifty years after the first telescope was made that men were shown what the surface of Mars might really be like.

The man to draw the first sketch of Mars was Huyghens. In 1659 his telescope showed him that nearly the entire surface of the planet was covered with an orange-red substance. He also noticed that it had large white patches at the north and south poles and that there were smaller patches of dark scattered over the planet. Another astronomer, Giovanni Cassini, in 1666, also noticed the Martian polar caps. So did Sir William Herschel, and Herschel went further than the others by pointing out that the polar caps became smaller and larger as the Martian seasons changed. Here was the first indication that the caps *might* be composed of ice or snow.

Schiaparelli's "canals"

It wasn't until 1877 that a really thorough study of the Red Planet's surface was made. And it was to set the astronomical world humming with excitement. The astronomer was an Italian named Giovanni Schiaparelli. Like Tycho, Schiaparelli was a careful observer and was devoted to his work. The year he made his first careful observation of Mars there were two important things in his favor. He had an excellent telescope. And Mars was due to pass very close to Earth.

Schiaparelli focused much of his attention on the Red Planet's dark patches, which astronomers then thought were seas. Like the others, Schiaparelli found no reason to think that they were not true seas. He reported that the seas were mostly brown. But sometimes, he said, parts of them looked gray and black; and these colored patches appeared to move around.

He reasoned that the Martian seas changed in appearance for the same reasons that our oceans on Earth change color. As the Sun moves higher and lower in the sky as the seasons change, our oceans become darker and lighter accordingly. Schiaparelli was sure that this explanation accounted for the changes in the Red Planet's seas. But today we know that what the Italian astronomer thought were seas are not true seas at all.

Schiaparelli also noticed changes in the land areas of Mars, areas he called "continents." While some appeared orange, others were a deeper red, and still others were yellow and nearly white. Some areas confused him. At times they appeared orange, then later changed to deep brown and to black. He couldn't decide whether they were continents or seas. Finally he concluded that they were swamplands which appeared to change color as their water level changed from season to season.

So far as the polar caps of Mars were concerned, Schiaparelli was convinced that they were composed of ice. Their melting during the summer and their new appearance each winter, he said, explained their marked annual change in size and shape. Schiaparelli's most startling finding about the mysterious Red Planet was its "canals," which we'll discuss in the next chapter. His announcement of the canals started astronomers on an argument which is still going on today.

One thing we should remember and be thankful to Schiaparelli for is that his studies of Mars created more interest in the Red Planet than has been created by any astronomer before or since his time. There is only one possible exception, the American astronomer Percival Lowell.

Lowell's dream

Like Schiaparelli, Lowell became a specialist on the planet Mars. In 1894 he set up an observatory in Arizona. The purpose of the observatory was to study the planets, but particularly the Red Planet. To this end the astronomer was devoted until his death in 1916.

Lowell was fascinated by the changes that took place on Mars' surface. Strongest in the astronomer's mind was the thought—life, human life on Mars, may be the cause of some of the changes we dimly observe from Earth.

There were two kinds of surface changes Lowell noticed. He saw very large areas, sometimes hundreds of miles across, expand and shrink over two- to four-year periods. Then there were other areas, *Lacus Moeris*, for example, which disappeared mysteriously and then for no apparent reason reappeared just as mysteriously. The second kind of change he noticed was easier to explain. They were most likely the same changes Schiaparelli saw in his seas. Lowell reported that certain areas changed from light to dark green, then to brown, and finally to yellow. He was certain that these changes were caused by the Martian seasons. He was also certain that Schiaparelli's seas were not bodies of water. They were lush fertile areas that abounded with vegetation and stood out in sharp contrast to the vast orange-red deserts.

In summer, Lowell thought, the ice caps melted and their water flowed into the dark areas and brought life to the vegetation. This accounted for the deep green color he observed. After their spring and summer growth, in the fall the areas of vegetation began turning brown and finally yellow, just as our own forests change color with the coming of winter.

Nearly all the observations Lowell made were directly associated with "life" to be found on Mars, whether it was intelligent life or simply a strange kind of Martian vegetation. And whenever Lowell mentioned Martian life, in the next breath he mentioned the elusive canals. For Lowell, the canals held the magic answer to the closely guarded secret of the Red Planet.

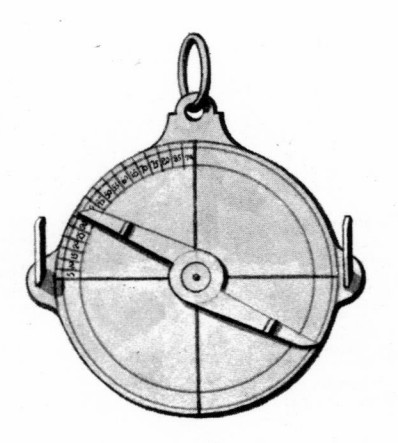

Stationed on one of Mars' jagged moons, you would have this view of the Red Planet which changes color with seasons.

canals on Mars

In 1877, the Italian astronomer Schiaparelli announced to the world that Mars was laced with a network of "canals." The canals, he said, carried water across the surface of the Red Planet in much the same way our irrigation ditches bring water to desert-dry regions of the Earth. This simple announcement of Schiaparelli's touched off an argument that raged for fifty years and is still going on today.

To many astronomers Schiaparelli's canals meant one important thing. If there were such canals, surely there were intelligent beings who built them. And considering the size of the Martian canals, the intelligent beings must have belonged to an advanced civilization, for the canals represented a tremendous engineering feat. If one of these canals were moved to Earth it would stretch from New York to Texas and would be one hundred miles wide! Perhaps you can understand why some astronomers hesitated to take Schiaparelli's canals seriously. Yet others did take them seriously.

The year the Italian astronomer discovered the canals was an exceptionally good time for observing Mars. The planet was swinging near Earth during one of its fifteen-year close approaches. And the telescope Schiaparelli used was a good one, even by today's standards.

Night after night as the astronomer watched Mars, he recorded on his drawings many thin lines which crisscrossed one another. Through the telescope they looked like dark furrows which seemed to connect the mysterious dark regions Schiaparelli had thought were seas. Always the canals ran straight and true, as though they were lines drawn by a draftsman. They never curved or twisted back on themselves as rivers sometimes do. Some of the canals were short and narrow and ran for only two hundred miles and were less than fifty miles wide. But others stretched several thousands of miles across the Red Planet and were sometimes one and two hundred miles wide.

Schiaparelli noticed two curious things about his canals. First, they seemed to be part of a plan. Each one he observed had a definite beginning and a destination which it always reached. They never ended in the middle of a "continent," the name Schiaparelli gave to what are now regarded as deserts. They always led from one dark region to another. Frequently two or more canals would meet at an unusually small dark area, then would continue as a single canal. These smaller dark areas Schiaparelli called "lakes."

The second strange thing Schiaparelli noticed was that from year to year, even from week to week, some of the canals seemed to disappear. Gradually they would change from their usual dark to a light color and finally would blend with the light surrounding land, and so "vanish." Other times a canal would mysteriously appear in a place where there had been none before. He explained the curious vanishing and appearing this way: In the spring and summer, as the polar caps melt, water flows into the canals. This gives them their dark color. Then as the water in a canal is soaked up by the ground and evaporated by the Sun, the canal turns a light color and so appears to vanish.

A few years after he first reported the canals, Schiaparelli announced that some of them had "doubled." The *Nilus* was one such doubling canal. Where previously there had been only one canal, suddenly two appeared. They ran side by side in straight lines, the second following exactly the same course as the original one. The distance between them was sometimes thirty miles. Other times it was four hundred miles. One day a canal would be single, then two or three days later it would mysteriously become double along its entire thousand-mile length. Sometimes the changes would take place within a few hours.

Such were the canals as Schiaparelli saw them. But the Italian astronomer wasn't the first one to report the canals, even though he is credited with discovering them. Drawings of Mars made in 1840 by W. Beer and J. H. Madler show lines resembling Schiaparelli's canals. So do drawings made in 1864 by the Reverend Charles Daws, a keen observer

Lowell said that Mars is crossed with hundreds of man-made "canals." Flying over the planet, this is the view you would have — if Lowell's description is accurate one.

known as "Eagle-eye." These men, however, made no attempt to explain the lines or give them names.

Calling the lines "canals" as Schiaparelli did is possibly the main cause of the great canal argument. When Schiaparelli published his findings they were written in the Italian language. And the word Schiaparelli used was *canale,* which means "channel," not "canal" in the English sense of the word. But English-speaking astronomers who were too anxious to criticize or praise Schiaparelli used the word "canal" and all it implies in English.

While astronomers the world over were arguing about Schiaparelli's canals, the Italian astronomer refused to take part in the debate. He never once claimed that the canals were made by intelligent beings. Yet he never once denied that they may have been built by "Martians."

Interestingly enough, many astronomers have never been able to see the canals. But others have and claim to have taken photographs which show them clearly.

As soon as Schiaparelli announced that there were canals on Mars, astronomers took up the search. But nine years were to pass before anyone reported seeing them. Perrotin and Thollon in France were the first to share the Italian astronomer's discovery. They found a canal on the night of April 15, 1886. Then on following nights they spotted others, some double, some single. And the canals they saw were located exactly where Schiaparelli had drawn them on his map of 1882.

Soon after the two French astronomers reported seeing canals on the Red Planet, astronomers in other parts of the world claimed they too could see them. They were H. C. Wilson in the United States, Stanley Williams in England, and F. Terby in Belgium. Many astronomers, however, were never able to find the canals, although they searched for several years.

How do astronomers explain this difference of seeing and not seeing the canals? A man with relatively poor eyesight cannot, of course, be expected to pick out fine detail as well as a man with excellent vision. Also, it takes many years of observing through a telescope before a man's eyes are trained for such fine work. Some astronomers say that once the canals are seen it's not difficult to spot them again and again later.

I remember as a child how my father tried time and again to show me the famous "White Horse," a trick image on the face of a cliff in New Hampshire's White Mountains. Patiently he would point out the forelegs, neck, and head, then he would ask, "Now do you see it?" Each time I had to confess that I didn't. Finally, after nearly twelve years of squinting and straining, I managed to make out the White Horse. In an instant it was there, clear and sharp. Possibly the Red Planet's canals elude astronomers in much the same way; and once they are seen, perhaps they stand out clearly the second and third times.

Lowell's canal theory

Lowell, the American astronomer, had no trouble finding canals on Mars. For nearly twenty years he was a devoted student of the Red Planet. Together with his staff he watched Mars from his fine observatory located in the clear desert air of Flagstaff, Arizona. In 1906 Lowell announced his now famous theory about Mars. The canals, he maintained, are vast artificial waterways built by intelligent beings. He was certain that the canals were not *natural* formations. In nearly every case they were straight lines connecting the shortest possible distance between two points. Therefore, they must have been made by intelligent beings, Lowell thought.

Until his death in 1916, Lowell stood by his canal theory, even in the face of bitter criticism from well-known astronomers. At his observatory he took several photographs which show the canals. Other canal photographs have been taken at the Lick Observatory in the United States and at the Pic du Midi in France. Among his many writings on the canals are two books, *Mars and Its Canals* and *Mars as the Abode of Life*.

Lowell's description of the Red Planet's canal system is very nearly the same as Schiaparelli's. But his explanation of the canals differs greatly. Lowell saw them as long, straight furrows forming a fine network over the planet's surface. At times the single furrows mysteriously doubled, running side by side like the tracks of a railroad. He said that the distance between the double canals varied greatly. While some were seventy-five miles apart, the distance between others was as much as four hundred miles.

Like Schiaparelli, Lowell said that sometimes two or more canals met at a common point, then continued on as one. While Schiaparelli called these points "lakes," Lowell called them "oases," for he was certain that Mars had been without large bodies of water for hundreds of years. This

Astronomers say that much of Mars is a sandy wasteland of red deserts. Wild wind storms are thought to rage, sometimes invading and covering areas of "vegetation."

leads us to the heart of Lowell's brilliant theory.

According to Lowell, Mars was once the proud possessor of a great civilization, perhaps even surpassing our own. There were cities like New York, London, and Paris; and there were lush, rambling areas of vegetation that colored the Martian countryside. Over the years, however, a

great tragedy was in the making. The planet's water supply was beginning to fail. At first the Martians found an easy solution to the problem. As we are doing in many of our big cities on Earth, they piped water in from distant areas. Gradually, over hundreds of years perhaps, they were forced to reach still farther and farther into the wilderness for their precious water. Finally, the problem became so serious that the planet's nations forgot their political differences and joined forces to achieve one thing only—self-preservation.

Realizing that the only source of water left to them was to be found in the melting polar caps, they began the mammoth task of digging a planet-wide irrigation system. By comparison, the construction of Egypt's pyramids was child's play. Possibly the Martians worked several hundred years to complete their giant system of waterways. But even when it was finished the planet was still doomed to destruction. For Mars was in its old age. Not only was its water supply nearly gone, but it was dying in other ways. Its free oxygen was also failing, so life on the planet was rapidly nearing an end.

Lowell's writings tell us that even today we can see the Martians' canal system in action. In the spring, as the polar cap melts, water fills the canals and flows toward the equator, bringing life to the few hardy plants and shrubs that managed to survive. As the canals become flooded they turn dark, and so account for the color change seen by Schiaparelli and others. As the life-giving water flows over the planet, vegetation along the banks of the canals springs into bloom. In this way each season the planet comes alive for a short time, then as the bitter Martian winter approaches, the canals dry up and the planet falls into a gentle sleep, waiting for the spring awakening.

During their latter days the Martians, according to Lowell, lived along the banks of the canals, where water would be nearby. And the "oases" where the canals meet are probably the remains of what once were proud Martian cities.

The canals, according to those who have seen them, stretch over the entire surface of the planet and lead in nearly every possible direction. If this is the case, Lowell's waterway system runs into difficulties. Unless you assume that every canal runs *downhill,* it's difficult to understand how the water gets from one point to another. Lowell got around this problem by saying that the Martians must have constructed an extensive pumping system that forced the water through the canals. He went even further by estimating how much power would be needed to pump the water. He decided that the power required would be four thousand times greater than that generated by Niagara Falls.

Today Lowell's writings tell us, we on Earth see the very last stages of life on Mars—the lingering vegetation which clings stubbornly in the planet's dying soil. We should consider ourselves fortunate, Lowell said, to be among the Earth dwellers who lived to see the remains of Martian life. For soon the last traces of life will be snuffed out on the planet and future astronomers will have to look to old photographs and drawings for what we have been fortunate enough to see firsthand.

That, in brief, is the heart of the brilliant astronomer's colorful theory of life and the canals on Mars. If you read Lowell's books you'll find it difficult to come away not believing at least parts of his story. The astronomers who disagree with Lowell do not question the logic of his theory. What they do question are the observations on which he based his theory. We must remember that Lowell's work on Mars was completed forty years ago. Many new things have been learned about the planet since then because larger and better telescopes have been made.

Some Martian experts today say that Lowell's maps of Mars look like cobwebs because of the great number of canals he drew. You would have a hard time to find any astronomer today who accepts Lowell's theory— that the Red Planet's canals were built by intelligent beings. In fact, you would have a hard time finding many astronomers who think that the canals are waterways—natural or artificial.

What, then, are the canals?

On one side are scientists who will tell you that they are nothing more than optical illusions, tricks that the eye plays on us. On the other side are those who think that the canals are natural surface markings, that they are really not fine, straight lines as some astronomers believed them to be. Instead, they are hazy streaks which have no such precise pattern as Lowell and others supposed.

Several years ago two men tried a "canal experiment" on boys about thirteen years old. The boys were given pencils and paper and were told that in a few minutes they would be shown something and that they were to draw exactly what they saw. The "something" was a circular piece of cardboard marked with light and dark patches, large dots, and other figures like those seen on Mars. When the drawings were finished and handed in, the two experimenters found that several of the boys had drawn lines connecting the dots and patches. And the lines were very much like those seen on astronomers' drawings of the Red Planet's canals. Yet there were no such lines on the cardboard disk the boys were told to copy.

31

What this experiment is supposed to prove is that our eyes play tricks on us, that we sometimes "see" lines that exist only in our minds. Here is an experiment that you yourself can try. Draw a series of small dots about an eighth of an inch apart on a sheet of paper. Now put the paper on the far side of the room and back away from it. When you're far enough away, the dots will blend and appear to be a solid line.

Once the Big Dipper and other constellations have been pointed out to us, we tend to imagine that straight lines connect the key stars, and so we form easily recognized images or patterns in our minds. And after we have looked at these constellations enough times it's very difficult for us to picture the stars as not being connected by lines.

W. M. Antoniadi and A. Dollfus, two well-known astronomers, both reached the conclusion that Mars' canals can be explained by the dot theory. When the seeing was fair and they were using small telescopes, both men saw the canals much as Lowell described them. But when the seeing was excellent and large telescopes were used, the lines of the canals were seen as a series of dots. Antoniadi's final words on the canals were: "The great telescopes of Meudon enabled me to settle once and for all the canal question."

Yet other astronomers also using large telescopes when the seeing is excellent insist that the canals are not mere tricks played by the eye. The canals stand out sharply and clearly, they say, just as they were pictured by Lowell.

By now you're probably wondering—Well, are there canals on Mars or aren't there? If you took a poll of the world's astronomers you might come up with this conclusion: There are markings on Mars which we will call "canals." But they are not natural or artificial waterways. They are not clearly defined lines running thousands of miles long. They are hazy, irregular lines which sometimes appear broken. They give no reason to suppose that intelligent beings are responsible for them. They are natural surface markings which have yet to be explained.

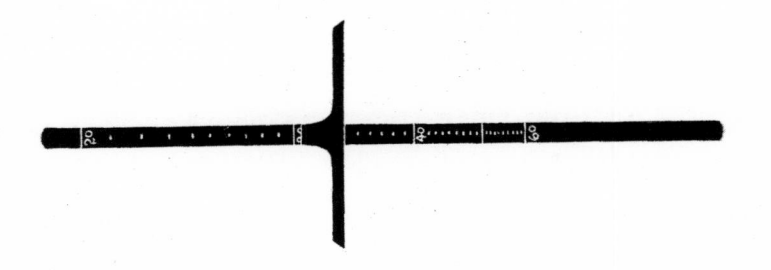

Mars is born

Before any biography is complete—even the biography of a planet—it's necessary to inquire into the parenthood of the subject. But discovering the parents of Mars is not as easy as it might seem. To answer the questions: Where did Mars come from? and How old is it? demands a wide search.

Kant's theory

One of the early theories explaining where Mars and the other planets came from was developed in the 1800's by a German named Immanuel Kant. Kant said that what is now the solar system was once a mammoth cloud of gas and dust, the thickest part being the center. Over millions of years the cloud "shrank" and formed individual globes which solidified to form the planets.

Jeans and Jeffreys

Sir James Jeans and Harold Jeffreys, two British astronomers, paint a different picture of how the planets were formed. These two men say that the planets were formed by a hit-and-run star. One time in the dim past, they say, an invader star from outer space rushed toward the Sun, grazed it, and continued speeding merrily on its way through the universe.

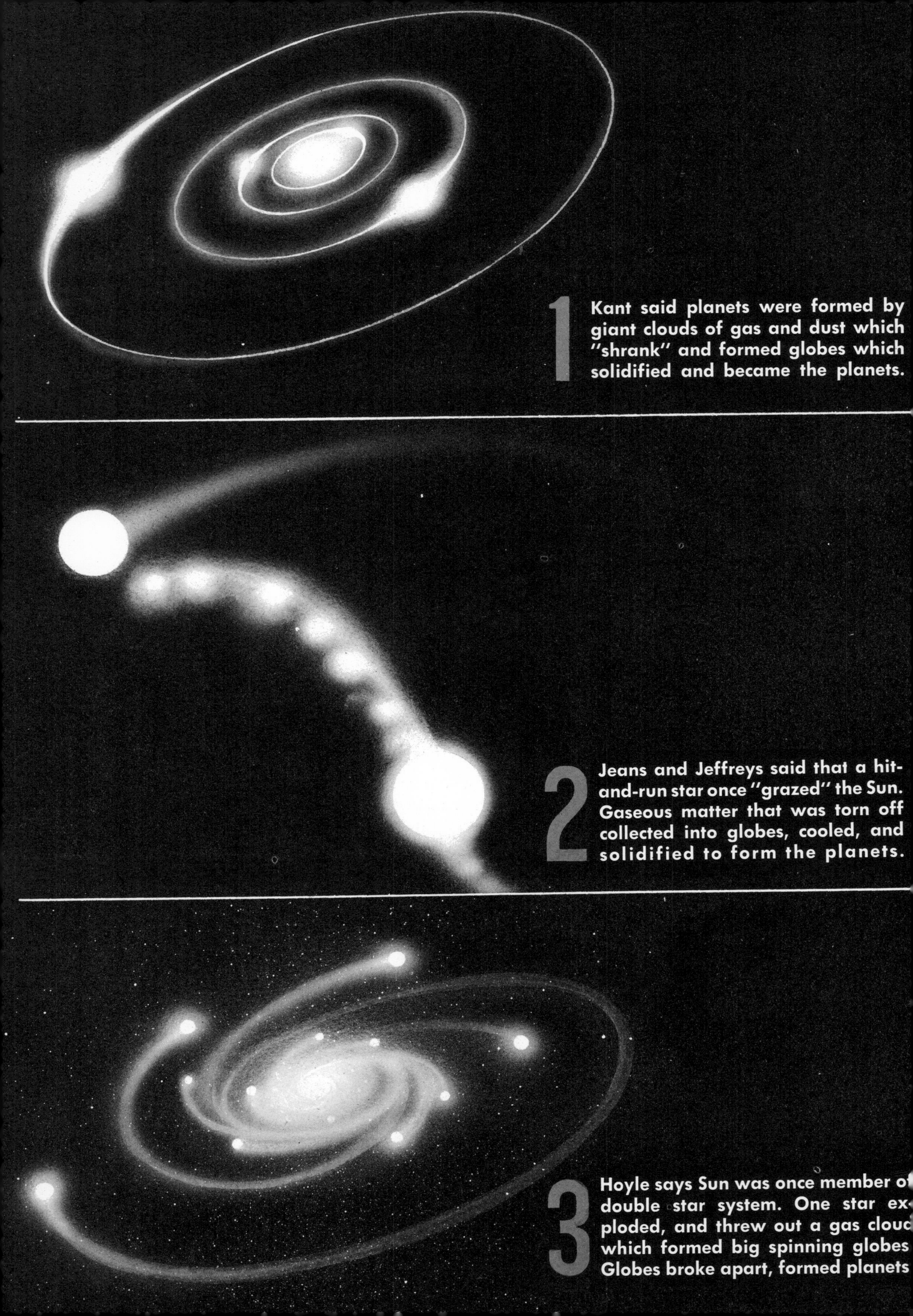

1 Kant said planets were formed by giant clouds of gas and dust which "shrank" and formed globes which solidified and became the planets.

2 Jeans and Jeffreys said that a hit-and-run star once "grazed" the Sun. Gaseous matter that was torn off collected into globes, cooled, and solidified to form the planets.

3 Hoyle says Sun was once member of double star system. One star exploded, and threw out a gas cloud which formed big spinning globes. Globes broke apart, formed planets.

During the stellar collision both bodies lost some of their hot surface matter, which flew off into surrounding space. Gradually the matter cooled and collected to form the planets.

If this is a true picture of how our planetary system was formed, it leads to an interesting thought. At that moment in cosmic history when the two stars collided, *two* planetary systems must have been formed, our own and one belonging to the invader star which carried its planetary system away with it.

As exciting as the Jeans-Jeffreys theory is, it cannot pass the test of recent astronomical fact, so we will have to look elsewhere for an explanation of the planet's origin.

More recently a number of other theories explaining where the planets came from have been proposed—one by Fred Hoyle and R. A. Lyttleton, two Englishmen; another by Carl von Weizsäcker, a German; and a third by Gerard Kuiper, who further developed Von Weizsäcker's theory.

according to Hoyle

Hoyle's theory is perhaps the most exciting one, but how accurate it is remains to be seen. He tells us that more than two billion years ago the Sun was a partner in a double star system. This means that two stars—our Sun and some other—were very close to each other. The other star, however, began to burn itself out. Eventually it exploded with such violence that nearly all of its matter was blown millions of miles into space. Only a small cloud of gas and dust remained near the Sun. Over a period of a few hundred years the cloud spread out around the Sun and formed a wide circular disk much like Saturn's rings.

Rapidly the tiny particles forming the disk began to cool. Slowly they were attracted to one another, collected into giant globes, and began rotating or spinning like tops. There were several of these giant globes, larger even than the great planets Jupiter, Saturn, Uranus, and Neptune. But something began happening to them. As they collected more gas and dust particles from the disk they grew even larger and spun faster. Eventually their speed of rotation was so great that the globes began to break apart, throwing chunks of matter throughout the solar system.

35

The larger chunks became the great planets—Jupiter, Saturn, Uranus, and Neptune. The smaller ones became Mercury, Venus, Earth, Mars, and Pluto. And even smaller ones became the moons of the planets.

Such is the exciting picture that Hoyle paints for us. But how much of it is true we don't know. While some astronomers think that Mars and the other planets may have been created this way, others turn to Von Weizsäcker for the answer.

what Von Weizsäcker says

Von Weizsäcker's and Kuiper's thinking about the planets takes us back to the gas-and-dust-cloud theory of Kant. According to these men, about four billion years ago our solar system was a vast swirling cloud of dust and gas having a mass ten times greater than the Sun. As it whirled around it flattened and formed a huge disk reaching out to Pluto, or to a distance of about four billion miles. Gradually, enormous whirlpools began to form in the disk. Where their edges touched, dust particles collected and began to form into tiny globes. Over a period of a hundred million years the globes grew until they reached enormous sizes and so became the planets. In many cases—the Moon, for example—smaller globes were "captured" by larger ones and became satellites of the planets.

The main differences between the Hoyle-Lyttleton and the Von Weizsäcker-Kuiper theories are (1) the amount of dust and gas in the original cloud and (2) how the dust collected to form the planets. While Hoyle and Lyttleton prefer the double star theory, Von Weizsäcker and Kuiper choose the dust-envelope explanation.

Many astronomers today think that the dust-envelope theory may be closer to the truth. Why? Because Hoyle's exploding star most likely would have sent most of its matter flying too far out into space. This would mean that only a small amount of matter would have been left near the Sun, too little to have led to the formation of all the planets.

It's possible that in ten years from now an entirely new theory will sway popular belief. It's also possible that men will *never* solve the puzzle of the origin of Mars and the other planets.

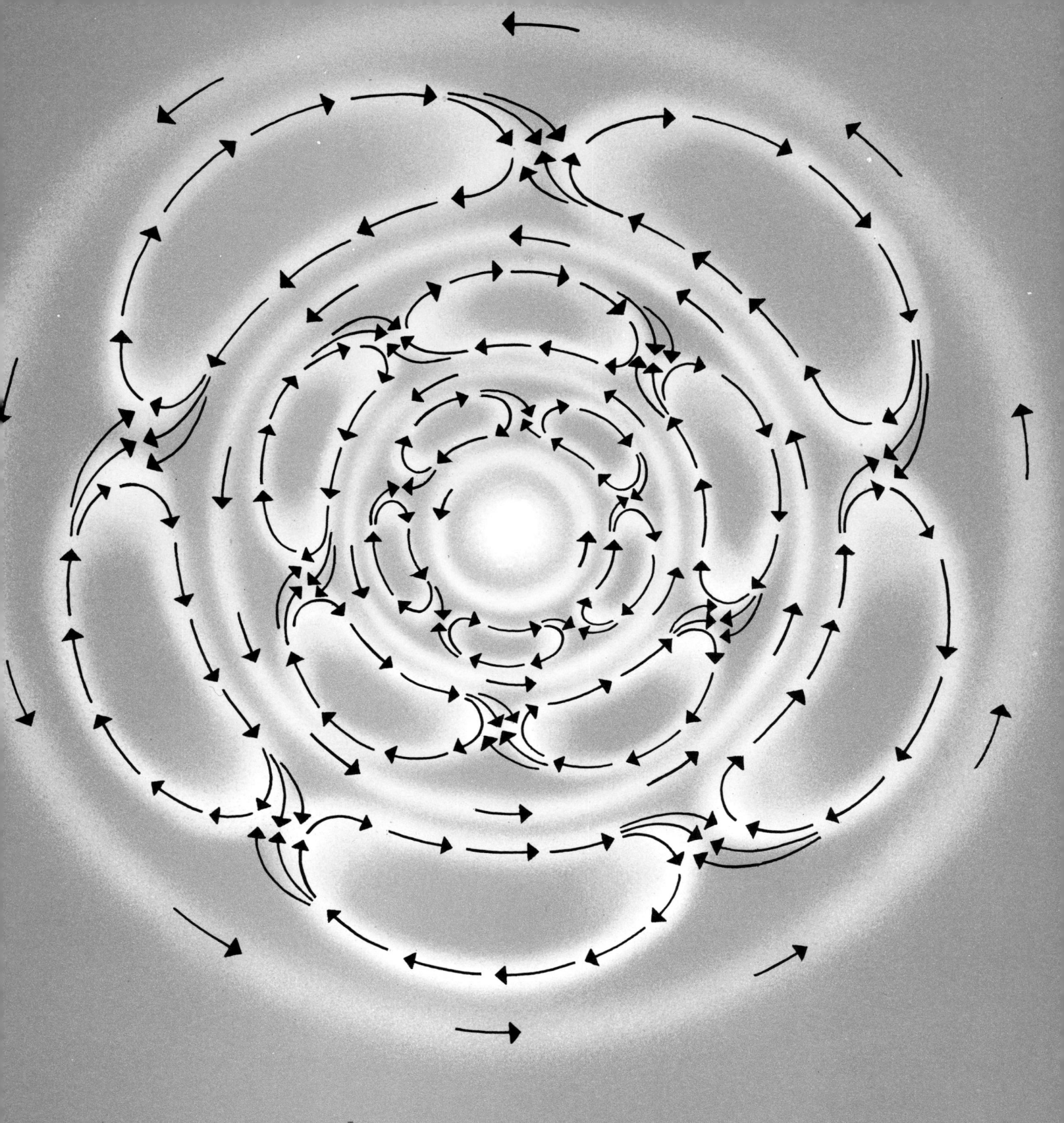

von weizsäcker's theory

The Sun's planets were formed out of swirling clouds of dust and gas. Where the clouds' edges touched (see diagram arrows) large gas and dust globes collected. Over millions of years the globes grew and hardened. Actual cause of planets' formation may never be understood.

exploring the red planet

As the title of this chapter suggests, we're going to take an imaginary trip to the Red Planet and try to find out what it would be like to live there. In some ways, life on Mars would be much the same as it is on our own planet. But in other ways, it would be frighteningly different—so different that after a few hours on Mars you'd lose no time in packing up and taking the next express rocket back to Earth.

your trip to Mars

If you made a trip to Mars on a super-fast express train traveling at 100 miles an hour both day and night with no stops, it would take you $40\frac{1}{2}$ years to reach Mars. Too long? Well, if you went by rocket traveling at 5,000 miles an hour, you could make the trip in about nine and a half months. Still too long? Well, a rocket going 20,000 miles an hour would get you there in two and a half months, provided there were no stops at satellite hamburger stands.

If you could someway pull yourself up to a position high above our solar system so you could look directly down on the Sun and its nine planets, you would see that Mars is the fourth planet out from the Sun. Mercury is closest to the Sun; next comes Venus, Earth, then Mars, the Asteroids, and the five outer planets.

Were you to plot the path, or orbit, Mars makes as it circles the Sun and compare it with Earth's orbit, you would notice a striking difference.

38

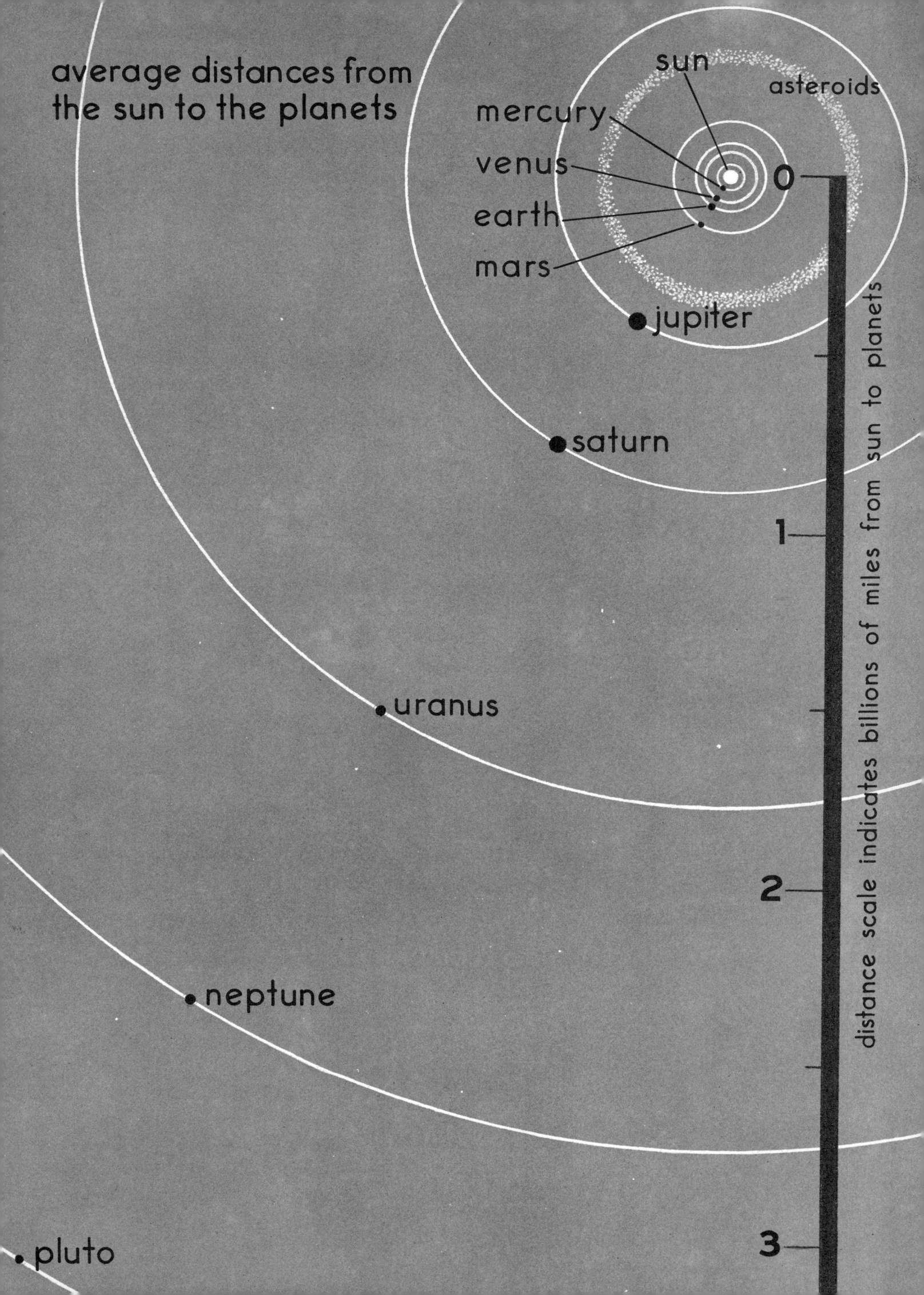

Whereas Earth's orbit is nearly circular, the orbit of Mars is a sweeping ellipse which looks much like a race track. Because of Mars' "long" orbit, the planet's distance from the Sun varies greatly. When closest to the Sun it is 128,000,000 miles away. And when it reaches the far end of its orbit it is 155,000,000 miles away. Taking an average of these two figures gives you Mars' "mean" distance from the Sun—about 142,000,000 miles. As

The orbits of earth and mars make up
a giant race track with earth on
the shorter path

earth

we all know, Earth is much closer to the Sun, its mean distance being only
93,000,000 miles.

The farther away a planet is, the more slowly it circles the Sun. While
Earth makes one trip around the Sun in a year, or in 365 days, Mars
takes nearly twice this much time—687 days, to be exact. So a Mars "year"
is about twice as long as an Earth year. If you lived on Mars you might

have trouble keeping track of your birthday, considering that you would have two every year.

Perhaps this will help you understand why astronomers can observe Mars only every two years. Look at it this way: Imagine two runners on a race track which is wide at one end but which is narrow at the other end and along the sides. Suppose that one runner goes twice as fast as the other. This would mean that the fast runner makes two trips around the track every time the slow runner makes only one.

Now think of Earth's orbit as the inside fence of the track, Mars' orbit as the outside fence, and the two planets as the two runners. Every two years and two months Earth, the fast runner, makes two trips around the track while Mars makes only one. In other words, Earth passes Mars once every two and one sixth years. It is during such passages, or "oppositions," when astronomers observe Mars, for the two planets are then side by side.

Now to complicate matters, every fifteen and seventeen years the two planets come exceptionally close to one another. This happens only when Earth passes Mars on the narrow section of the track. At such times the two planets are only 35,000,000 miles apart. When Earth passes Mars on the wide-end section of the track, the planets are 62,000,000 miles apart.

telling time on Mars

When you make your first trip to the Red Planet you'll have to buy a special Mars watch or take your own to a jeweler and have it adjusted. The reason is that the length of a Mars day is twenty-four hours, thirty-nine minutes, and thirty-five seconds. The forty-minute difference in time is so slight that you probably wouldn't notice it, but if you failed to correct your Earth watch, which is set for a twenty-four-hour day, you would soon run into difficulties, particularly if you had to be on time for an important meeting.

42

Martian seasons

Once we adjusted our lives to a slightly longer day, we would next have to get used to the long Martian seasons. This might be difficult at first. Mars has seasons, because, like Earth, the Red Planet is tilted on its axis. At certain times of the year this enables the Sun to shine more directly on some parts of the planet than it does on other parts. On Earth our seasons last about three months, or ninety days each, but since Mars takes nearly twice as long to circle the Sun, its seasons are nearly twice as long as ours. Fall to winter on Mars lasts 146 days. Winter to spring, 160 days. Spring to summer, 199 days. And summer to fall, 182 days. A winter in Siberia must be mild in comparison with a Martian winter!

Not too long ago astronomers regarded Mars as a deep-freeze planet, thinking that its temperatures were nearly always below freezing. But recent temperature measurements of the Red Planet paint a less frigid picture.

Since Mars is farther out from the Sun than Earth is, we would expect to find Martian temperatures colder than ours. But how much colder, no one was sure until Seth B. Nicholson and Edison Pettit at the Mount Wilson Observatory and W. W. Coblentz at the Lowell Observatory measured the Red Planet's temperatures by using an instrument called the thermocouple. Although these measurements were made in the 1920's they are considered quite accurate today, even though astronomers now use better instruments to measure the temperatures of the distant planets.

If you took a sight-seeing trip across Mars, here are the hot and cold areas you could expect to pass through. At the equator of the planet at high noon the temperature would be in the neighborhood of 75° F., what we would consider balmy spring weather. Moving up to the North Pole, the mercury would plunge sharply to 94° F. below zero. But by going to the opposite end of the planet, to the South Pole in summer, you could bask in the sun and watch your thermometer register a comfortable 50° F. If you decided to cross one of the Red Planet's large deserts, you would be fairly comfortable, for the desert temperatures range from 15° F. to 40° F. And on entering one of the planet's dark green areas you would be even more comfortable in temperatures that would rise to 50° F., 68° F., and sometimes as high as 85° F.

On Earth the day's heat usually becomes highest around midafternoon, but not so on Mars. Water vapor or moisture in the Earth's atmosphere acts as a blanket and stores up the heat of high noon, so we feel it most around three o'clock. But scientists have discovered that Mars has very little water vapor in its atmosphere. For this reason Martian temperatures climb highest at noon, then begin to fall immediately after twelve o'clock. Because the planet's atmosphere stores very little heat, the air becomes extremely cold the instant the Sun sets. By midnight you would be fighting cold in the region of 150° F. below zero!

During your sight-seeing trip across the Red Planet you would soon discover that you feel strangely lightweight. The fact is, you would weigh less on Mars because the Red Planet's mass—or the amount of matter it is made of—is less than Earth's. If you weigh 100 pounds on Earth, you would weigh only 37 pounds on Mars. Many people wonder if this low surface gravity would seriously curb our activity. Not at all. In fact, most of us would feel a new sense of "freedom" and would adjust to our lightness after two or three days. We'd be able to move around with much less effort than we use on Earth. Also, we wouldn't tire so quickly or so easily. Frequently we'd feel as though we were actors in one of Hollywood's slow-motion pictures. All objects would seem to float through the air, moving slowly as though they were in a world of make-believe. In many respects Mars' surface gravity, which is only about a third of ours on Earth, would provide us with many pleasant and amusing experiences. Try to imagine a baseball game on Mars. Nearly every hit would be a home run!

deserts and mountains

Mars is a small planet compared with Earth. Its diameter is only 4,200 miles, a little more than half that of Earth and twice the diameter of the Moon. In spite of its smaller size, Mars has just about the same land area as we have on Earth, since three-quarters of the surface of our globe is covered by oceans. Mars is without oceans, lakes, and rivers.

If you ever look at Mars through a telescope, you'll notice that about two thirds of the planet is covered with brightly colored patches, some as large as our continents. They range in tints from brick red to deep rose to bright orange. Even with the naked eye Mars is seen to glow with this characteristic red color.

Most astronomers today think that the vast orange areas are deserts, much like our own famous Sahara Desert. Or they could be vast areas of flaky stone. The red coloring may be the surface remains of a planet that

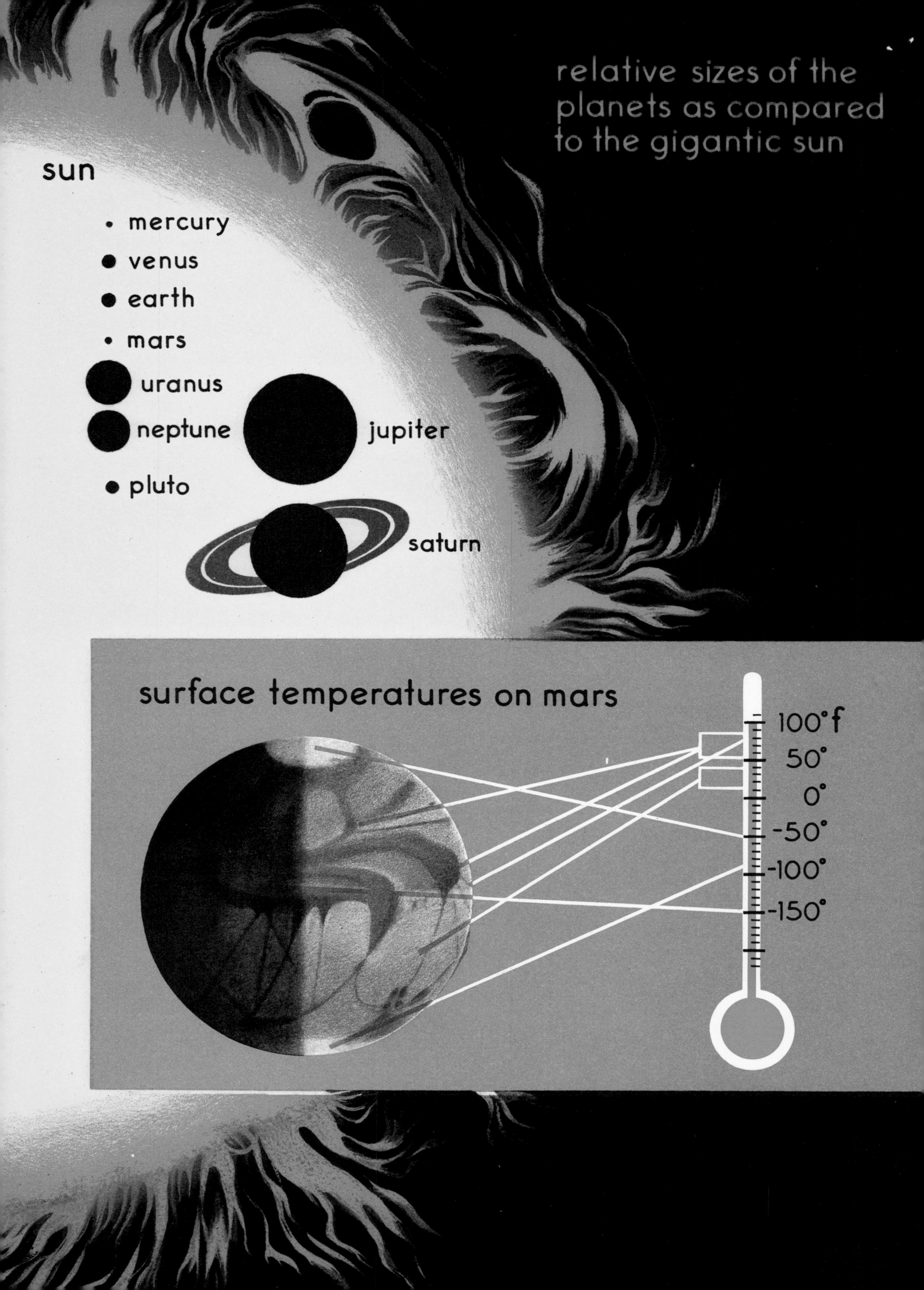

relative sizes of the
planets as compared
to the gigantic sun

sun

• mercury

• venus

• earth

• mars

uranus

neptune   jupiter

• pluto

saturn

surface temperatures on mars

100°f
50°
0°
-50°
-100°
-150°

has rusted itself to death. Many astronomers believe that once in the Red Planet's history its free oxygen combined with sand and rocks to produce a rust-like substance resembling the sands of the spectacular Painted Desert in Arizona.

As beautiful as a trip across a Martian desert might be, it probably would become extremely boring after a day or so. Unlike Earth and the Moon, the Red Planet has no impressive mountains which would provide a contrast after a long drive over the desert. If Mars had even one or two majestic peaks like the Alps or the Rockies, our telescopes could find them. At sunset they would cast long shadows that would stand out prominently. But no such shadows have ever been detected on Mars. If the planet does have mountains, they probably are not higher than five or six thousand feet. Some observers, however, have reported mysterious white dots which are always seen in the same position. They suspect these dots may be the tops of low mountains capped with snow or ice.

the great dark areas

The Red Planet's mysterious dark regions are nearly as prominent as its painted deserts. Seen through a telescope, they appear as great broad patches several hundred miles wide. Sometimes they are varying shades of gray. Other times they are a deep forest green, and still other times a light green of new grass. Exactly what these dark regions are and what causes them to change color aren't known, but astronomers have been willing to make some bold guesses about them.

Every competent observer of Mars has seen the dark regions and doesn't rule out the possibility that they may be rambling beds of plant life something like our own here on Earth. As we mentioned earlier, Schiaparelli and some of his followers supposed that the dark regions were oceans and lakes, but about 100 years ago this idea was abandoned. And with it was abandoned the hope that bodies of water of any impressive size will ever be discovered on the Red Planet.

46 Lowell and other observers have noticed that the dark regions on Mars undergo two different kinds of changes. The first change can be compared with the growth of our deserts or the change in shape of a volcanic mountain. Each of these changes takes place gradually and over a long

period of time. The Martian area called *Mare Cimmerium* is an example of such a long-range change. In 1800, 1924, 1937, and 1946, astronomers noticed that the northwest shore of this dark region had expanded. Similar changes have taken place in another area known as the *Solis Lacus,* or "Lake of the Sun." And more recently a desert-like area about the size of Texas mysteriously took on the dark color of "vegetation" regions.

The second kind of change astronomers see in the dark regions is considered a seasonal change. In the summer certain dark areas begin to broaden and stretch out into the surrounding bright desert regions. Then as winter sets in these same regions withdraw, returning to the same shape and size they were before winter. Seen from another planet, the Earth would display similar changes in its large forest areas and grassy plains.

The French astronomer Gérard de Vaucouleurs, Antoniadi, and others have noticed seasonal changes in a Martian region known as the *Syrtis Major.* In 1909, 1926, 1941, and other years, this area spread gradually east toward *Libya* and *Moeris Lacus* during autumn and southern winter; then with the coming of southern spring, the area returned to its former shape.

Seasonal changes like the one seen in *Syrtis Major* take place so regularly that astronomers can predict them quite accurately.

There are still other changes that take place in the dark regions. The French astronomer G. Fournier has seen dark areas around the Martian polar region become broader and darker with the coming of the summer. Slowly they creep toward the equator, each year following the same general plan. Appearing as huge gulfs, they grow along certain canals at a speed of one half to eleven miles a day; and within a few weeks they completely change the appearance of the surrounding landscape. One of the outstanding dark regions of this type can be seen in the area known as the *Hellespontus.*

Seasonal changes even more spectacular than these have been reported. With the coming of Martian spring, observers see certain areas change to a bright green, then with the arrival of the summer Sun they turn a darker green; and finally, as winter approaches, the areas exhibit rich yellows and browns. This change suggests that Mars may well have vegetation akin to our trees and shrubs, which undergo the same color changes with the approach of new seasons. Some astronomers deny that they have ever been able to observe such color changes, but Lowell and

47

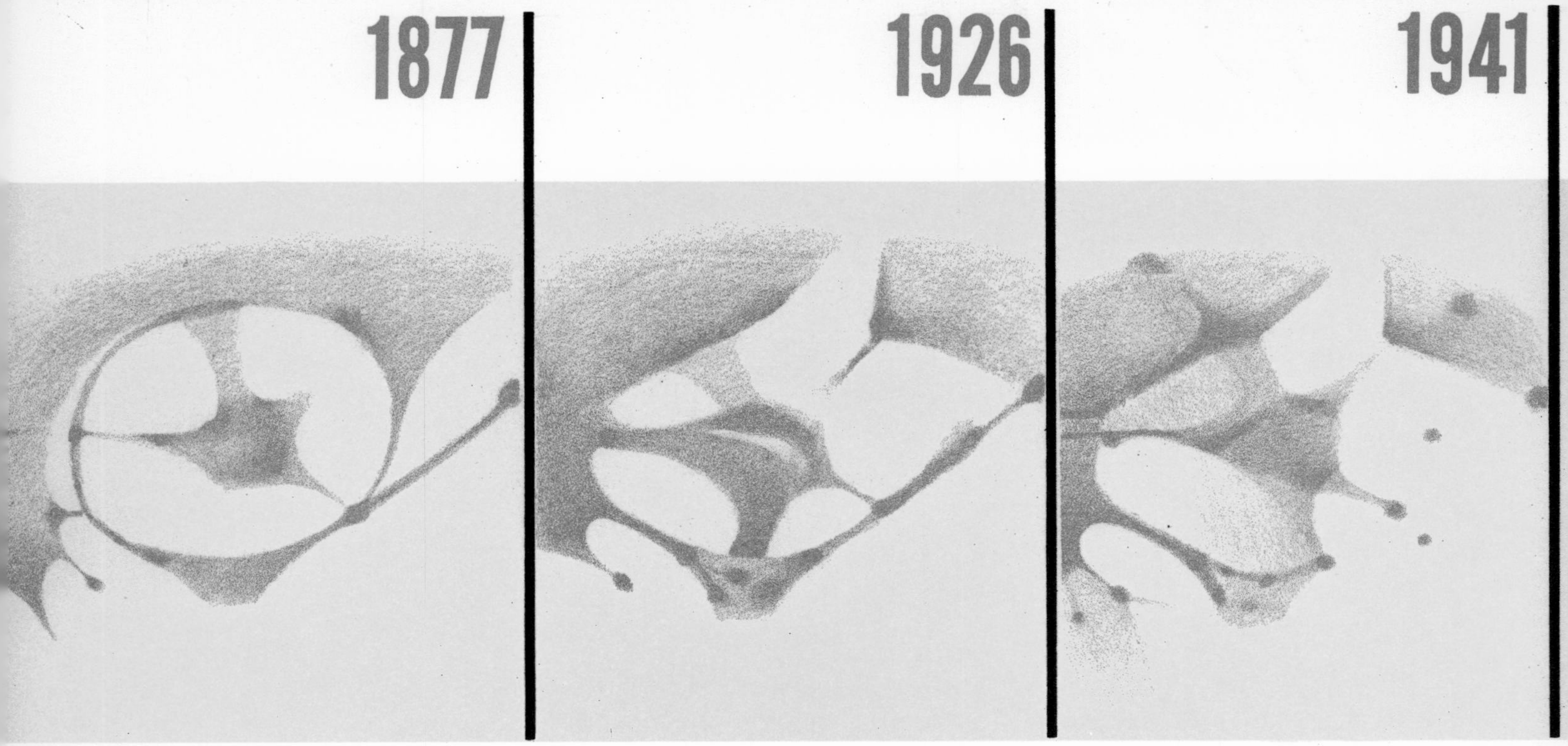

1877　**1926**　**1941**

Solis Lacus: Like other areas of Mars, the Solis Lacus has undergone changes. Surrounding dark areas appear to close in and choke off the lighter regions. Eventually, many such areas return to former shape.

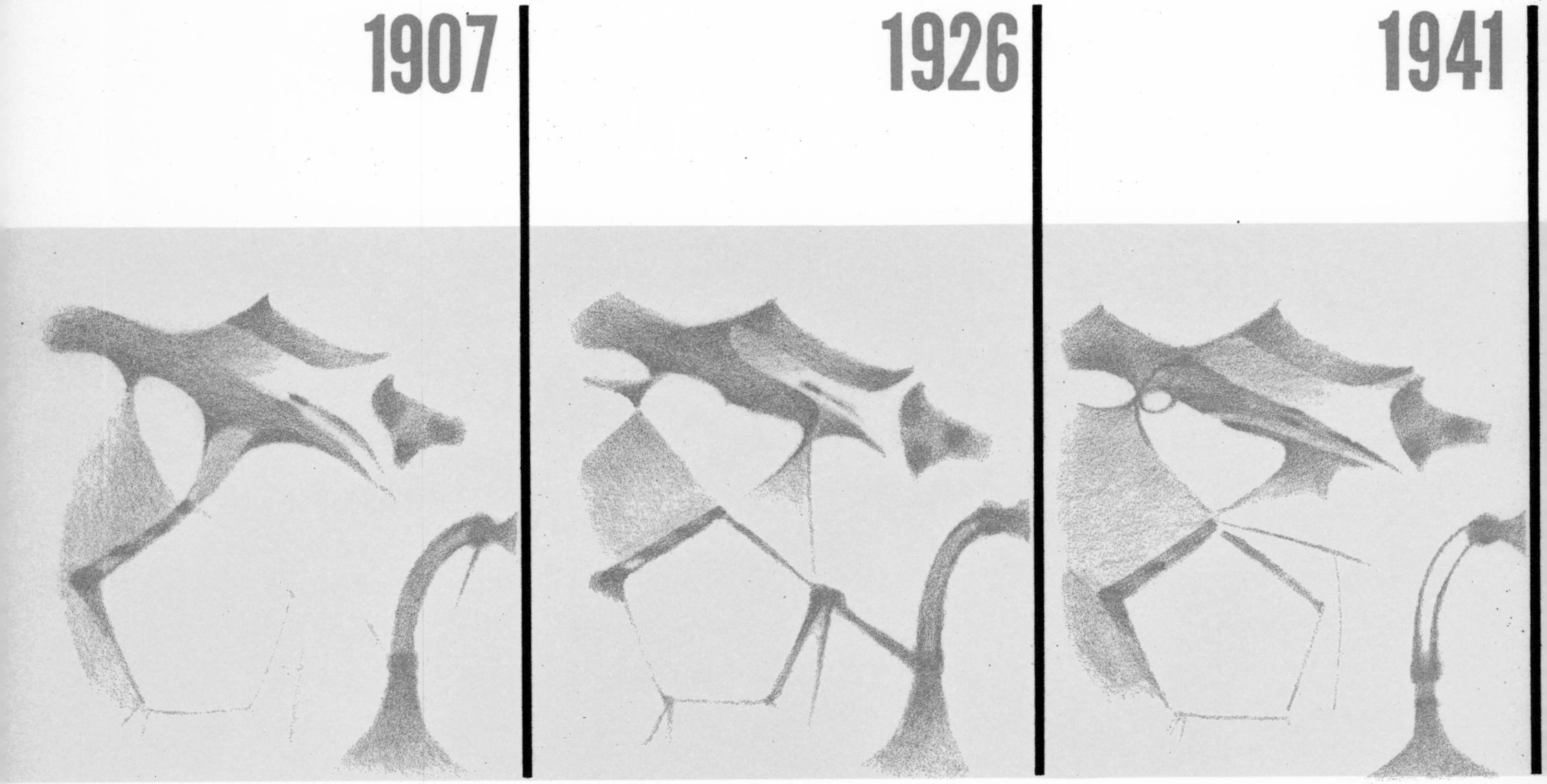

1907　**1926**　**1941**

Mare Cimmerium: This is another area where changes have taken place. The diagram shows how at three different periods the north-west shores of Mare Cimmerium have been seen to change their shapes.

others insisted that they occur with regularity.

One of the most startling dark area changes in more than 100 years was reported after the Red Planet's passage in 1954. Photographs taken at Mount Wilson, and by the veteran Mars observer E. C. Slipher, show the following picture: in one Martian year a broad land area twice the size of Madagascar and located close to the *Thoth-Nepenthes* canal has changed from a desert to a dark area. Previously *Thoth-Nepenthes* was hazy and hard to find, but now it stands out sharply.

Changes like these raise two questions: (1) Do they mean that there is some kind of life on Mars? And (2) What causes these areas to change? A look at the Martian polar caps may hint at an answer to these questions.

polar caps

For as long as astronomers have seen the gleaming white areas at the North and South poles of Mars, they have thought of them as having some influence on the great dark areas. Gérard Kuiper at the Yerkes Observatory and others have recently concluded that the polar caps are definitely made of snow which melts during the summer, then forms again during the winter. Years ago, some astronomers thought that the polar caps were nothing more than large clouds hovering above the polar regions.

If you watched Mars through a telescope every night as the planet passed through one of its seasons, this is what you would see. During mid-spring in the Southern Hemisphere the great south polar cap (which spreads over four million square miles) begins to break up. Slowly great cracks appear, beginning at the edges, and as they broaden, small islands of snow are created. As the spring thaw continues, the hub of the polar cap shrinks more and more. Finally, at the end of summer the main cap appears to be on the verge of disappearing completely. But it remains, and as winter sets in it begins to grow again and becomes intensely white as it reaches its full impressive size, extending nearly halfway to the equator.

It would seem that the Martian polar caps are thick fields of snow, much like Earth's caps of ice which build to hundreds of feet in depth. But astronomers doubt this. Surprisingly enough, even in midwinter the Martian polar caps are probably no more than a few inches thick. They

49

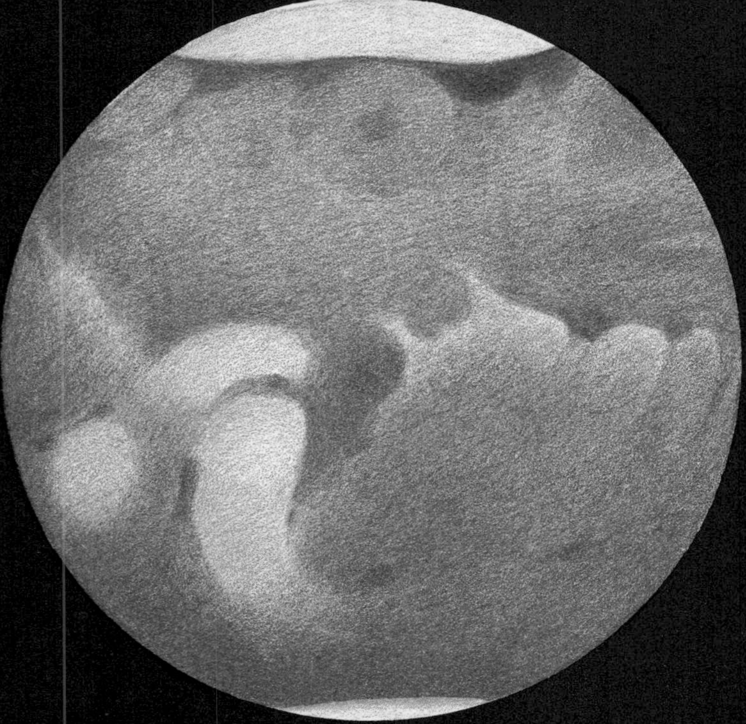

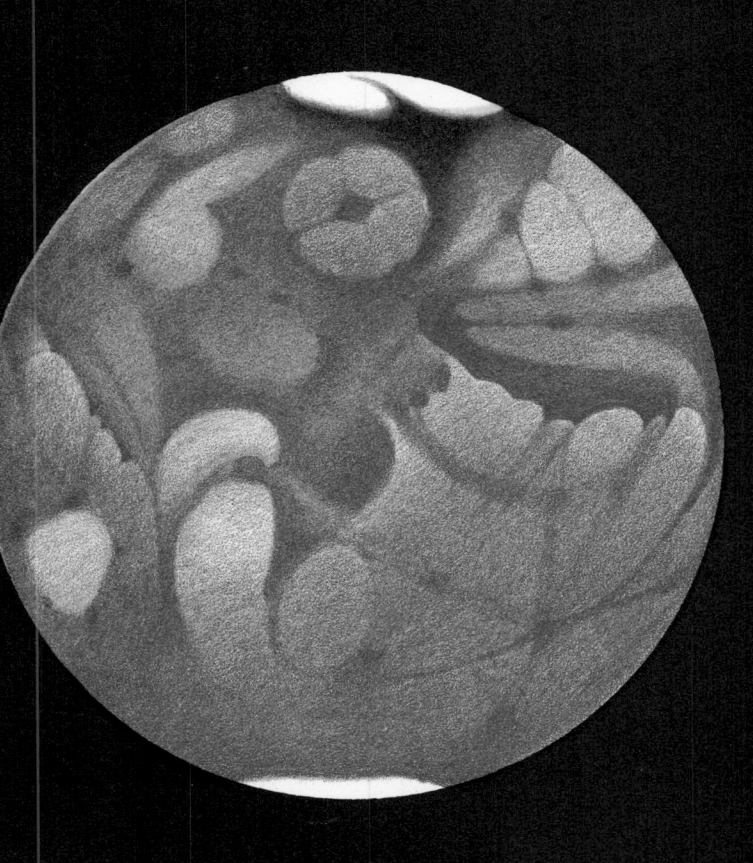

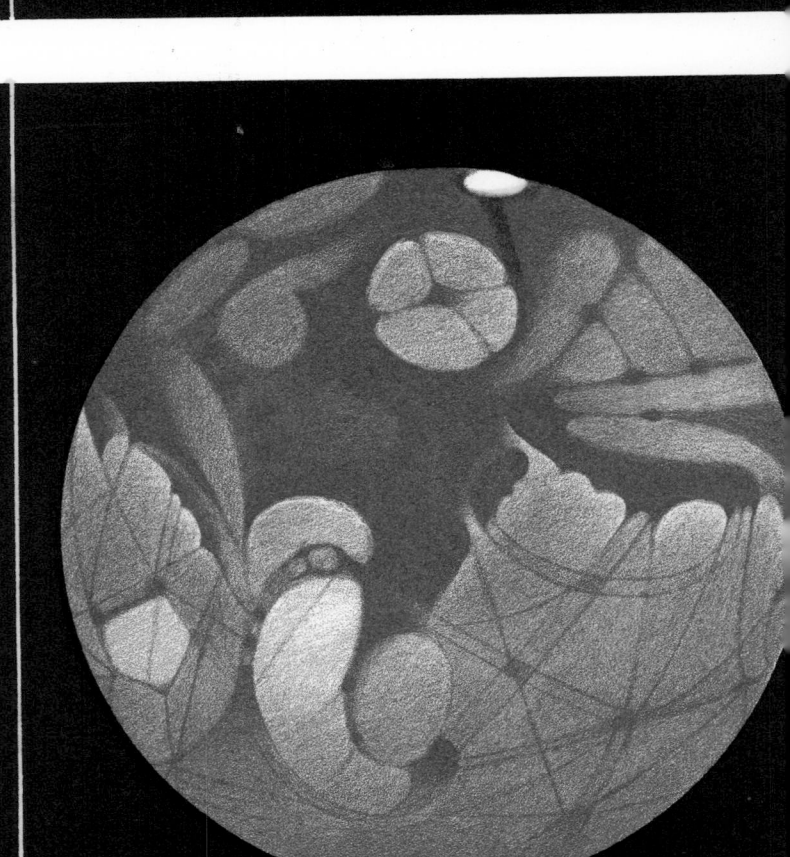

1 Winter: As Martian seasons change, astronomers can see marked changes taking place on planet. In these drawings notice how polar cap grows small as spring, early and late summer set in.

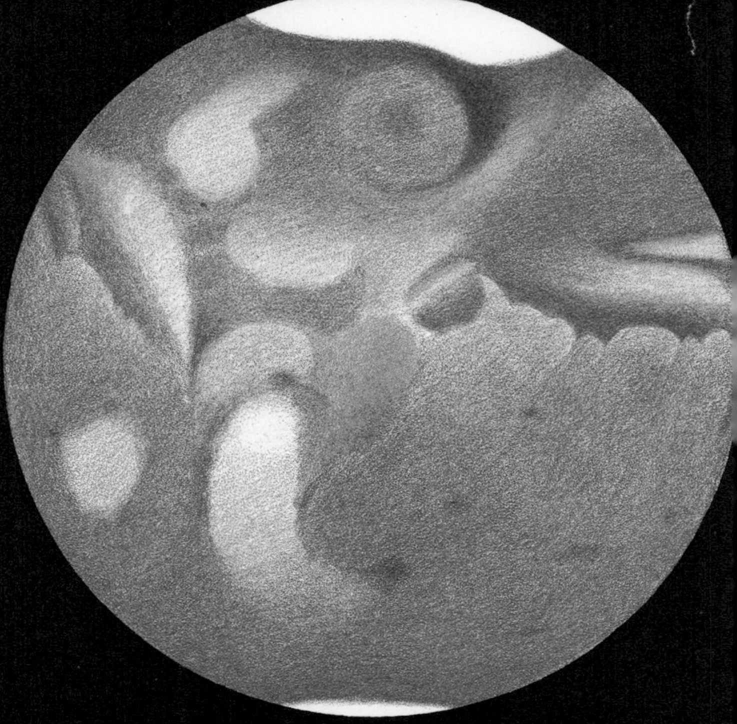

2 Spring: During spring thaw dark regions near polar cap and near planet's equator begin to spread out. Astronomers think that melting ice of polar cap flows into areas of "vegetation."

3 Early summer: By this time of the Martian year many canals bloom into sight. Some dark areas begin expanding at rate of 1 to 11 miles daily. Within weeks nearby land changes completely.

4 Late summer: Polar cap is nearly gone. Canals become sharper, dark areas turn a deep brown like forests on Earth. At the end of fall, brown and yellow colors fade and polar cap enlarges.

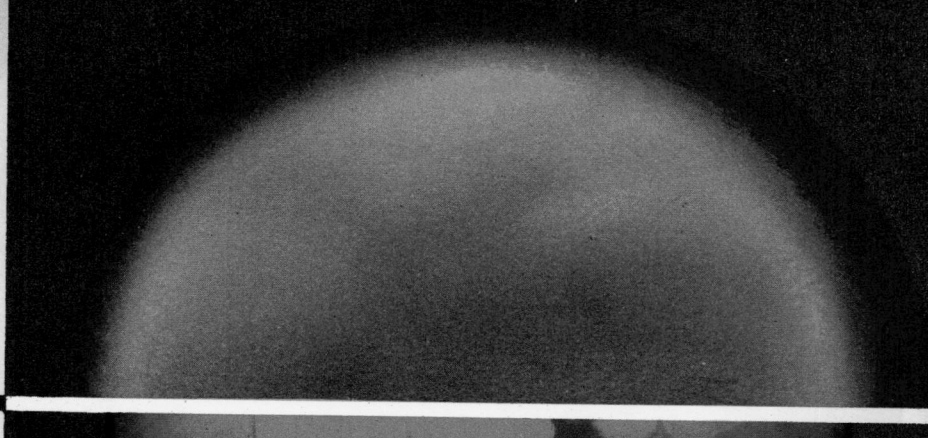

Ultra-violet light photographs show Mars as fuzzy disc. What the camera records is envelope of air surrounding the Red Planet.

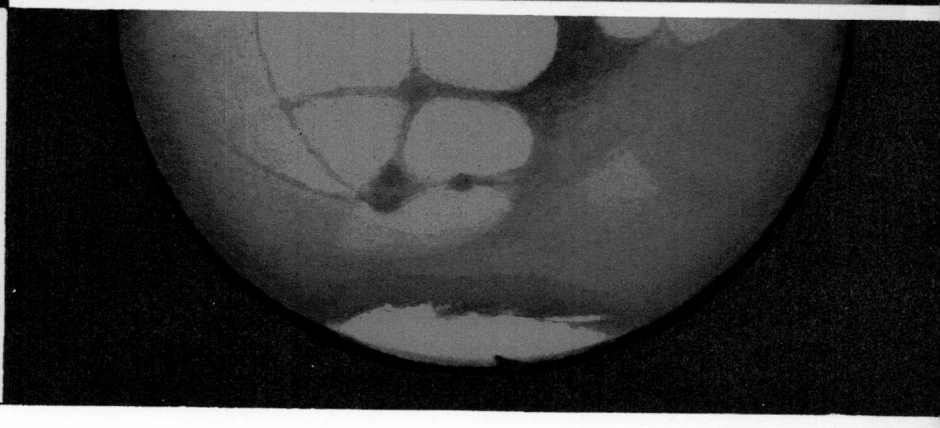

Infra-red light photograph shows surface of Mars, not atmosphere. By comparing both photos, depth of planet's air is revealed.

break up and re-form again so regularly that astronomers can predict quite accurately when and to what extent they will change.

A baffling question about the polar caps is: What happens when they melt? The meager supply of water could seep into the surrounding areas, or it could evaporate into water vapor and become part of the planet's atmosphere.

Astronomers suspect that it may do a little of each. But in what proportion, they are not at all sure. Since Mars has a very thin atmosphere, it cannot hold much water vapor. In short, it cannot hold all the moisture that would come from the evaporation of one of the planet's polar caps. So a certain amount of the snow must melt and seep its way into the Martian soil. Reaching outward, it creeps toward the planet's equator, and as it moves it causes many changes in the color of the lands around the polar regions.

A sound understanding of the nature of the Red Planet's polar caps —exactly what happens to them when they disappear each season— would help clear up several of the Martian mysteries.

the red planet's air

51

Before 1930, astronomers pictured the Martian atmosphere quite differently from the way we picture it today. Some men were convinced that the Red Planet's air was very much like our own. Oxygen and water vapor, they thought, were plentiful enough to allow a man to live as comfortably on Mars as he can on Earth. This hopeful but inaccurate picture of the Red Planet's atmosphere led some astronomers to nod approvingly at Lowell's magnificent canal theory.

In 1934 and 1937, however, astronomers using up-to-date means of viewing the atmospheres of planets announced a new set of findings.

The news left little doubt that the Red Planet's atmosphere has neither oxygen nor water vapor in abundance. In fact, Mars most likely has less than a thousandth of the oxygen present in our own atmosphere. And water vapor is probably just as scarce.

Then what is the atmosphere of Mars made of?

Gerard Kuiper, working at the McDonald Observatory in Texas, has discovered carbon dioxide in the air of the Red Planet. Other astronomers reason that there also must be small amounts of argon, neon, and other rare gases. So the general picture of Mars' atmosphere is possibly something like this: a great deal of nitrogen (which makes up four fifths of our atmosphere), some carbon dioxide (possibly twice the amount in our air), traces of argon, and *very* small amounts of oxygen and water vapor.

Astronomers collect most of their knowledge of the Martian atmosphere by taking photographs of the Red Planet. But it isn't an easy kind of photography. First, by using a special filter they take a picture which shows the planet bathed in ultra-violet light. When the film is developed it shows a fuzzy disk which is actually the envelope of air that encloses the planet. Next, by using a different filter they take a picture displaying the planet in infra-red light. When this film is developed it shows a clear outline of the planet's surface. On this photograph the atmosphere of the planet is invisible. By comparing the sizes of the two images they can tell how high into the Martian sky the atmosphere stretches. This distance is about fifty or sixty miles, only a third of the depth of the Earth's atmosphere.

If you spent several nights at the telescope and carefully watched Mars, you would find that the Red Planet has clouds much like those we have in our own atmosphere. Mars' clouds, however, appear only yellow and white through the telescope. They are too far away to reflect the beautiful desert sunset colors.

52

The morning sky of Mars is usually clear. But around noon puffy white clouds begin to appear, small at first, then they grow larger. You can see them best in the late afternoon, two hours or so before sunset. These white clouds are thought to be moisture produced as the afternoon temperatures fall sharply. Usually they hang high in the Martian sky, sometimes twelve miles above the planet.

The yellow clouds are more difficult to see. They tend to blend with the yellowish-orange color of the Martian landscape. Generally they hang low over the ground and sometimes remain for several weeks in the same area. Their strange behavior may mean that they are mammoth sandstorms raging over the deserts. Yet some astronomers suggest that they might be clouds of dust and ash coming from Martian volcanoes.

But this raises another argument. Can there be volcanoes on Mars? What we know about volcanoes tells us that they occur near water and in areas of recent mountain building—at least if we are to judge all volcanoes by those that occur on Earth. And since Mars has neither large bodies of water nor impressive mountains, it seems doubtful that volcanoes exist on the planet.

But Dean B. McLaughlin of the University of Michigan thinks that Mars does have volcanoes. In fact, he suggests that many of the Red Planet's dark areas are extensive beds of volcanic ash and that the areas change in shape as the volcanoes erupt every now and then. Four Martian volcanoes, McLaughlin says, are located in the areas of *Pambotis*

Some astronomers think volcanic ash explains the dark regions on the Red Planet.

Lacus, Hydaspis Sinus, and in *Solis Lacus.* He also tells us that the marked changes seen in the *Thoth-Nepenthes* canal are caused by an extremely active volcano in the *Alcyonius Nodus* oasis. Much more research will have to be done before we know for sure whether or not Mars has volcanoes.

the red planet's moons

For many years astronomers supposed that Mars was without a moon. Textbooks and technical papers written about the planet stated flatly that Mars has no moons.

But an astronomer named Asaph Hall refused to accept the textbook view. He had no reason to think that Mars *did* have a moon, yet no one had ever proved that the Red Planet was moonless. Hall decided to find out for himself.

For most of the month of August 1877, he painstakingly searched the sky around Mars. Night after night he watched the Red Planet, but he failed to see anything resembling a moon. Discouraged and annoyed with the poor seeing conditions, one night Hall decided to abandon his search. But before quitting he took one last look. Within minutes he sighted something—a tiny body so close to Mars that it was extremely difficult to see. Just when he got it fixed in his telescope, fog settled in and made seeing impossible.

For the next five nights clouds kept Hall from his telescope. Impatiently he waited for them to clear. Finally, on August 16, the seeing was again good. Excitedly he returned to his telescope. The tiny object was

54

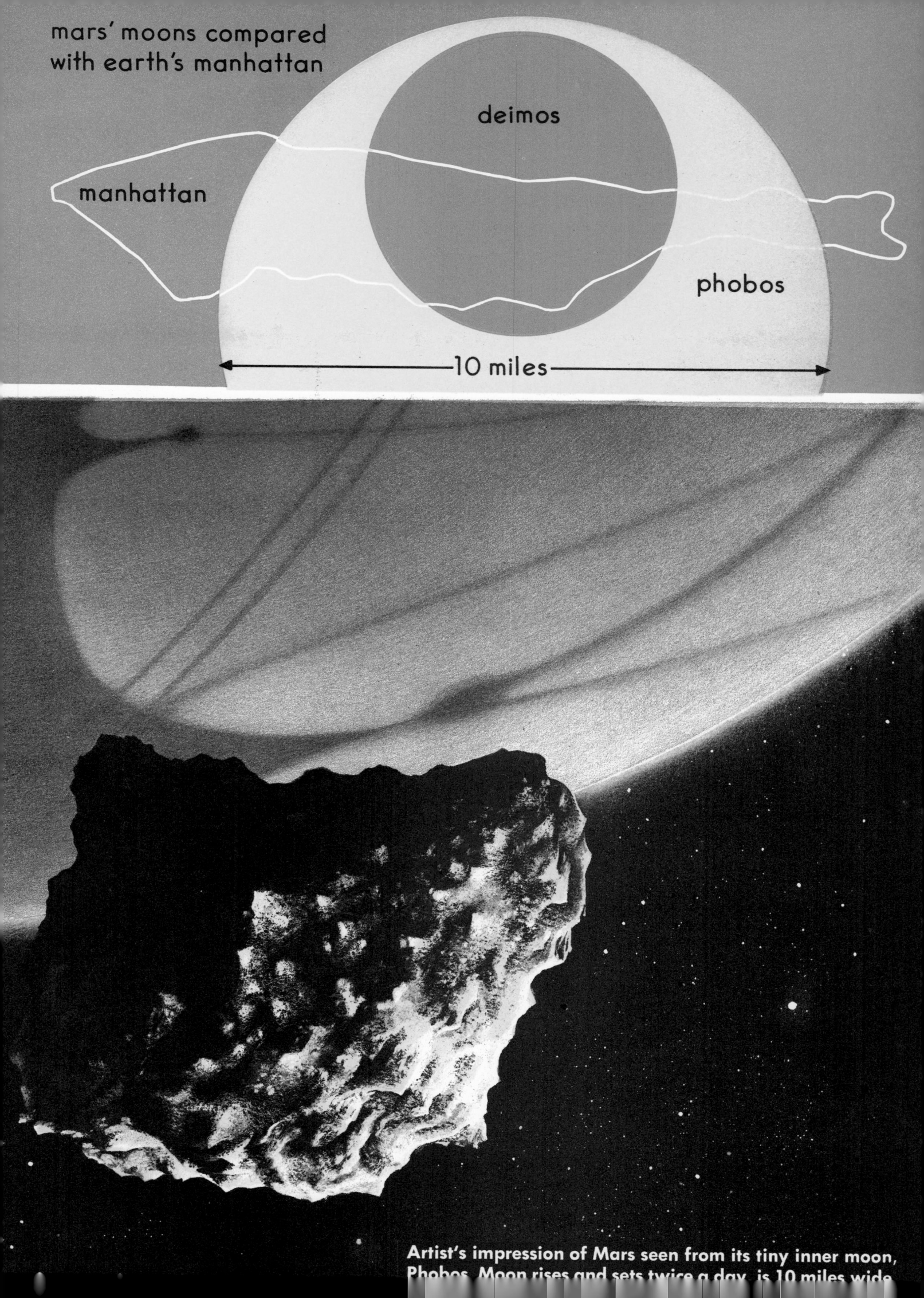

mars' moons compared
with earth's manhattan

deimos

manhattan

phobos

10 miles

Artist's impression of Mars seen from its tiny inner moon,
Phobos. Moon rises and sets twice a day, is 10 miles wide

still there. Furthermore, it moved along with Mars and so revealed itself as a true moon. Hall was overjoyed at his discovery, but the following night he had cause for even more joy. He discovered a second moon. Unlike the first, the second moon was circling the planet with such speed that Hall decided it must rise in the west and set in the east, a unique event in the entire solar system. Hall decided to name the outer moon Deimos, which means "panic," and the inner moon Phobos, which means "fear." These were the names of the two companions of Mars, the "God of War" in Roman mythology.

Deimos is the smaller of the two moons. Astronomers think that it is only five miles in diameter, so small that from Mars you would see it as a star, not as a bright disk like our own Moon. Deimos' speed around Mars is so slow in relation to Mars' rotation that the moon takes sixty hours to rise and set.

Phobos, the inner moon, is a real speed demon, taking only seven hours and forty minutes to circle the planet. This means that you would see it rise and set twice a day, taking only four hours and eighteen minutes between the time it popped over the horizon and dropped out of sight on the other side of the planet. In addition to being faster than Deimos, Phobos is thought to be about twice as large, having a diameter of about ten miles.

The size and shape of the Red Planet's moons are not at all certain. It's quite possible that they are not circular like our Moon. Instead they may resemble a large mountain which somehow had been uprooted and flung out into space to become a moon.

Mars may well have other moons in addition to Deimos and Phobos. But if it does they are probably so small that they will remain undetected until the first space ship crosses the 35,000,000 miles separating Earth from its mysterious red neighbor.

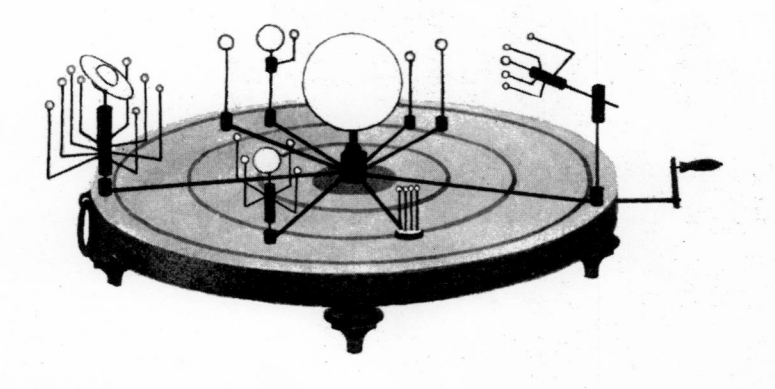

life on Mars

the great Martian invasion

On the night of October 30, 1938, thousands of people across the country were peacefully enjoying dance music coming over their radios. Suddenly a voice interrupted the music:

"Ladies and gentlemen, we interrupt our program of dance music to bring you a special bulletin from the inter-continental radio news. Twenty minutes before eight, central time, Professor Farrell at the Mount Jennings Observatory, Chicago, Ill., reported observing several explosions of incandescent gas occurring at regular intervals on the planet Mars. The spectroscope indicates the gas to be hydrogen and moving toward the Earth at enormous velocities. Professor Pearson of the observatory at Princeton confirms Farrell's observations and describes the phenomenon as 'like a jet of flame shot from a gun.' We now return you to the music of Raymond Rafiella playing for you at the Meridian Room of the Park Plaza Hotel situated in downtown New York. . . ."

After a few more minutes of music the program was again interrupted:

"Ladies and gentlemen, following on the news given in our bulletin a moment ago, the government meteorological bureau has requested the large observatories of the country to keep an astronomical watch on any further disturbances occurring on the planet Mars. . . ."

A third announcement told the radio audience that a large "meteor-like" object had crashed on a New Jersey farm and that it was being examined by scientists. An on-the-spot radio news reporter described the object as a "huge cylinder" with a diameter of thirty yards. In the background, police sirens and a noisy crowd could be heard. The news reporter suddenly became panicky as he described what was happening to the cylinder. Slowly the top opened, and out of it a strange "ray gun" appeared. It shot flames which burned and killed several hundred spectators and Army troops standing by.

Several minutes later a strange metal object on three telescopic legs rose out of the cylinder and began marching over the countryside. Its flame thrower destroyed buildings and killed everyone in its path. Meanwhile, other such machines with Martian invaders inside were reported to be waging destruction across the entire country and in Canada. The "jets of blue flame" seen on the planet Mars were part of the army of Martian rocket ships on their way to invade and conquer the Earth.

I remember this dramatic radio show vividly. I was fifteen at the time and recall how excited our neighbors were. Many of them believed that this Orson Welles radio drama was true. The following day newspapers all over the country reported the mass hysteria the program caused throughout New York and New Jersey. Thousands of people fled from their homes. For miles around New York City the roads were jammed. As I recall, there were some deaths caused by the panic. For an hour or two during that memorable night of October 30 there were millions of people who were convinced beyond a doubt that there was life on Mars.

It would be interesting to find out how many people would be fooled by such a drama if it were broadcast today. Probably there would be few —unless the program were done on television! Then there might be a nationwide panic.

For some reason people like to think that there is life—human life—on Mars or on some other planet in our solar system. A number of times I have heard friends say in effect, "I know that there aren't any 'people' on Mars. But wouldn't it be nice if there were!" It's odd that many of us hold a strong hope that one day human life *may* be discovered on some other planet, if not in our own solar system, then in some other. Perhaps it's because man doesn't like to think of himself as being alone, as being unique in the universe. He wants company, even if the company is millions of miles away, and even though he may never live to know that company. Somehow, it's comforting to think that perhaps *somewhere* in the universe there are other people like us.

58

How do you go about deciding if there is life "out there," untold millions of miles away from our tiny planet? If you were asked to deliver a talk on this topic, where would you start?

A short time ago I was invited to take part in a discussion about science and science-fiction writing. There were three of us who led the discussion—the head of a large publishing house, a well-known science-fiction novelist, and myself. Our audience was made up of about thirty people, mostly teen-agers with a sprinkling of adults. Eventually the discussion worked its way around to flying saucers. Are there actually flying saucers? And are they invaders from outer space?

Since I had written a number of magazine articles debunking flying saucers, I was asked to start the discussion. I began by saying that in two or three minutes any scientist could make mincemeat of the so-called "authoritative" books supporting the wild theories of flying saucers. I tried to explain that we cannot talk intelligently about life on other worlds if we know nothing about the other worlds. And the worlds we know something about—Mars and the other planets in our solar system—cannot possibly support a high form of life capable of navigating space ships around the cosmos. By the time I finished I was confident that I had won the audience. But then it was the science-fiction novelist's turn.

He said that simply because we know nothing about other worlds in space, why shouldn't we assume that they support "a strange form of life—intelligent life?" Then he went on to paint pictures of weird "vegetable men" who communicate by mind reading, creatures who can make themselves invisible, and still others who can transport themselves through time and space simply by willing it. So colorfully did he speak of his never-never-land creatures that the audience all but forgot my argument.

Whenever we talk about life on Mars or any other planet, we must begin with what we know—not with what we don't know. The scientist would laugh at the "vegetable men" theory, or if he had a sense of humor he'd say that on Mars a vegetable man would be a deep-freeze vegetable, and on the Moon he'd be a vegetable stew!

are there Martian "human" beings?

In earlier chapters we learned that (1) there is exceptionally little water on Mars; (2) there is practically no free oxygen in the Martian atmosphere; (3) there is even less water vapor; (4) the planet has a daily temperature range of about 200°—meaning that at midnight the human body would have to fight temperatures of 150° F. below zero, then in a few hours adjust to a warm temperature of 50° F. above zero; and (5) most of the planet is a vast, hostile desert.

Knowing that the human body needs lots of oxygen, water to drink, water vapor to breathe, and "comfortable" temperatures, we must conclude that there are no Martian "human beings."

could there be animals?

Even on the remotest sections of Earth, animal life abounds. When we cross any of our great deserts, all appears to be still and lifeless, yet beneath the hot sands there is life. There are spiders, snakes, and small rabbit-like creatures, to mention a few. Only a few inches beneath the sands the temperature remains nearly constant the year round. Isn't it possible, then, that some low form of animal life may one day be found on Mars?

Even if Martian animals could escape the severe cold of Martian nights by burrowing underground, how could they survive in a world with so little oxygen and water? We know that some of the lower animals can adapt themselves remarkably well to severe conditions, so it would be a mistake to say flatly that animal life cannot possibly exist on Mars. On the other hand, we cannot say that there is animal life on the planet. We can only admit it as a remote possibility.

is there plant life?

If there is animal life on Mars there would certainly have to be plant life. For animals cannot live without plants; but plants can live without animals.

Like animals, plants need oxygen and water if they are to survive. If you've ever examined plants closely—even desert cactus—you know that you can squeeze water out of them. Can you imagine what would

60

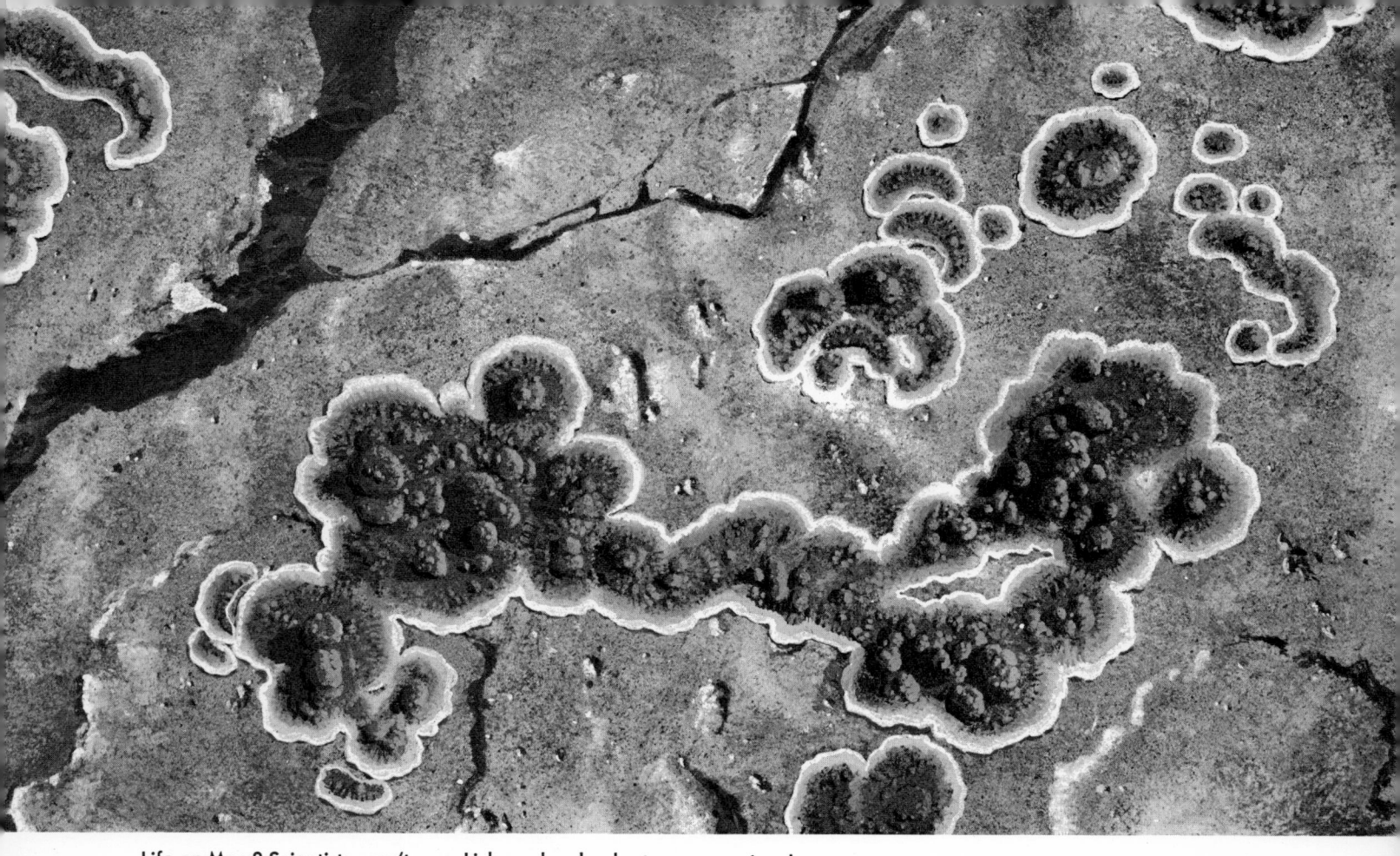

Life on Mars? Scientists aren't sure. Lichens, hardy plants, may survive there.

happen to such a plant on Mars? At night, when even the summer temperatures plunged far below zero, the water in the plants would freeze, expand, and kill the plant. Such is the gloomy picture some astronomers paint.

But G. A. Tikhov, a Russian scientist, is much more hopeful about Martian plant life. For many years he has studied plants that live high up on mountains, in areas where the temperature is nearly always at freezing and where the humidity is near zero. His reports show that more than two hundred varieties of plants abound in these hostile areas, which he says must be very much like Mars. Since many plants seem to adapt themselves to severe conditions, we should by no means rule out Martian plant life, the Russian scientist tells us. They *can* survive the cold. They *can* live on very little water. And they *can* manufacture their own oxygen and store it in their roots.

One kind of plant—the lichen—may find Mars an extremely healthy place to live. In fact, the Martian "areas of vegetation" may possibly be extensive, rambling beds of lichen growth.

61

Lichens are a strange plant which survives nearly impossible conditions on Earth. You find them growing in the cold of Siberia, on sun-baked stone walls, on desert rocks, and on bare mountain peaks. While some of them look like scales, others are like moss and long, tangled masses of thread. They come in nearly every color imaginable—red, green, yellow, brown, and blue-black. These strange plants manufacture their own oxygen and require very little water for survival.

As inhospitable as the Martian world appears, our lichen friends would possibly find life there quite pleasant. While some astronomers prefer to think of the Red Planet's areas of vegetation as lichen growth, others refer to the areas simply as "some kind of plant-like life."

This description of "life" on Mars is a far cry from the imaginative picture of Martian life created by Lowell and writers of science fiction. For Lowell, the strange and mysterious markings we see on Mars today represented the dying embers of life. In them he saw the last visible remains of what thousands of years past may have been a great civilization, before the planet lost its oxygen supply. In his thrilling book, *Mars as the Abode of Life*, Lowell left his reader with these words:

To our eventual descendants life on Mars will no longer be something to scan and interpret. It will have lapsed beyond the hope of study or recall. Thus to us it takes on an added glamor from the fact that it has not long to last. For the process that brought it to its present pass must go on to the bitter end, until the last spark of Martian life goes out. The drying-up of the planet is certain to proceed until its surface can support no life at all. Slowly but surely time will snuff it out. When the last ember is thus extinguished, the planet will roll a dead world through space, its evolutionary career forever ended.

How is it possible to deny Lowell his great dream—that in ages past Mars was an "abode of life"? The telescope and other modern instruments are pitifully inadequate to answer the probing questions we have about Mars. They can tell us many things, but they cannot answer what we think of as the most important questions.

Possibly within our lifetime these questions will find their answers, when the satellite program leads the way to interplanetary travel. When that great day arrives, teams of archaeologists, biologists, physicists, and astronomers will go to Mars. And within a few weeks they will once and for all solve the enticing mystery of the Red Planet.